The Battle of Castillon 1453

The Death Knell for English France

Peter Hoskins

Helion & Company Limited
Unit 8 Amherst Business Centre
Budbrooke Road
Warwick
CV34 5WE
England
Tel. 01926 499 619
Email: info@helion.co.uk
Website: www.helion.co.uk
Twitter: @helionbooks
Visit our blog http://blog.helion.co.uk/

Published by Helion & Company 2023
Designed and typeset by Mary Woolley, Battlefield Design (www.battlefield-design.co.uk)
Cover designed by Paul Hewitt, Battlefield Design (www.battlefield-design.co.uk)

Text © Peter Hoskins 2023
Illustrations © as individually credited
Colour artwork drawn by Giorgio Albertini © Helion & Company 2023
Maps by George Anderson © Helion & Company 2023

Every reasonable effort has been made to trace copyright holders and to obtain their permission for the use of copyright material. The author and publisher apologise for any errors or omissions in this work and would be grateful if notified of any corrections that should be incorporated in future reprints or editions of this book.

ISBN 978-1-804513-55-2

British Library Cataloguing-in-Publication Data.
A catalogue record for this book is available from the British Library.

All rights reserved. No part of this publication may be reproduced, stored in a retrieval system, or transmitted, in any form, or by any means, electronic, mechanical, photocopying, recording or otherwise, without the express written consent of Helion & Company Limited.

For details of other military history titles published by Helion & Company Limited contact the above address or visit our website: http://www.helion.co.uk.

We always welcome receiving book proposals from prospective authors.

Contents

Acknowledgements v
Preface vi

1   The Hundred Years' War: Causes and the Ebb and Flow of Fortune
    to the Treaty of Tours in 1444   7
2   The Military Reforms of Charles VII   23
3   Evolution in Artillery During the Hundred Years' War   28
4   An Uneasy Peace, The Truce of Tours 1444–49   40
5   The Reconquest of Normandy 1449–50   46
6   The French Conquest of Gascony: The First Campaign   66
7   John Talbot, First Earl of Shrewsbury   78
8   The French Conquest of Gascony – The Second Campaign   88
9   The Battle of Castillon, 17 July 1453   94
10 The End of English Aquitaine   108
11 Aftermath   117

Colour Plate Commentaries   121
Bibliography   123

Acknowledgements

I am particularly grateful for the expert advice of Doctor Guilhem Pépin on several matters relating to the history of Gascony during the English presence. He provided me with some invaluable sources and clarified ambiguities relating to names of people and places. My thanks go also to Paul Hitchen, Nicolas Savy, Charles Singleton, the Groupe d'Archéologie et d'Histoire de Blanquefort, and Alain Parbeau for permission to use their images and to Andrew Vallance and Michael Horah for their very helpful reviews of the draft text.

Preface

The English victories at Crécy (1346), Poitiers (1356) and Agincourt (1415) are prominent in English folklore and memory. However, few are familiar with the defeat of John Talbot, 1st Earl of Shrewsbury, and the Anglo-Gascon army on 17 July 1453 at Castillon on the River Dordogne, 25 miles east of Bordeaux – the last of the great battles of the Hundred Years' War. Castillon heralded the rapid collapse of English power in South-West France, and three months later the last English soldiers left Bordeaux. The battle brought to an end a series of rapid campaigns which, in a little over four years, had driven the English from their lands in Normandy and Gascony, leaving the Calais Pale as the only surviving possession in France – a possession that the English Crown would hold for another 100 years. The battle also marked an important step in the evolution of warfare. King Charles VII had brought about major reforms in the French army, establishing a standing army and, thanks to the technical and tactical innovations of the Bureau brothers, at Castillon, artillery played a decisive role on the battlefield for the first time in Western Europe.

French Handgunner, c.1450
(Paul Hitchen)

1

The Hundred Years' War: Causes and the Ebb and Flow of Fortune to the Treaty of Tours in 1444

The Hundred Years' War

Castillon, like all the great battles of the Hundred Years' War, means little out of the context of the broader history of the war, particularly as the strategies adopted by both sides evolved throughout the war. It was only in the nineteenth century that historians adopted the term 'the Hundred Years' War' to cover the conflict between the kings of England and of France between 1337 and 1453. The term is somewhat misleading, since it gives the impression of a period of continual warfare, whereas there were several distinct phases of war, interspersed by periods of truce and peace, and the strategies employed varied between these phases.

The English strategy in the reign of Edward III (1327–1377), from the outbreak of war in 1337 until his death in 1377, was largely one of mobile warfare through mounted raids, called *chevauchées*. There were numerous sieges, most notably those of Tournai in 1340 and Calais in 1346–7, but, overall, the objectives of the strategy were to take the war deep into enemy territory and to bring the French to battle, but only if the circumstances were right, rather than attempting to occupy territory. This strategy also served to demonstrate that the King of France was incapable of fulfilling his duty of defending his people. The strategy has been described by the historian Clifford J. Rogers as being focussed on people rather than places.[1] Under Henry V, and until the end of the war, the emphasis of English strategy

---

1 Clifford J Rogers, *War Cruel and Sharp, English Strategy Under Edward III, 1327–1360*, (Woodbridge: The Boydell Press, 2000), pp.307–8.

changed. Bringing the French to battle was still an objective, but taking and holding towns to establish English rule became the prime objective. For the French, the major successes of Charles V (1364–1380) in driving the English out of the territories ceded by the Treaty of Brétigny of 1360, and of his grandson Charles VII (1422–1461) in finally expelling the English, were largely attributable to the retaking of towns and fortresses and the re-establishment of French rule in those lands previously under English rule.

The Causes of the Hundred Years' War

There were two underlying causes of the war that started in 1337: the homage claimed by the French kings from the Kings of England for their lands in France and the English claim to the throne of France.

The anomaly whereby English kings were sovereign in England but were in frequent dispute with French kings over homage for their lands in France can be traced back to William the Conqueror who, after his victory at Hastings in 1066, was both King William I of England and Duke of Normandy. The situation was exacerbated when Henry II came to the throne in 1154, since he had acquired extensive lands in South-West France through his marriage to Eleanor of Aquitaine two years before and thus he, and subsequent English kings, also ruled the Duchy of Aquitaine, centred on the city of Bordeaux. The status of Aquitaine was a constant cause of dispute between the Kings of England and of France, with the French kings demanding homage from English kings who, in turn, proclaimed their right to full sovereignty as Dukes of Aquitaine. In the years immediately preceding the Hundred Year's War there were protracted diplomatic wrangles between Edward III and Philippe VI about homage. Matters came to a head in 1337, with a dispute over the extradition from England of a French exile, Robert of Artois, one-time adviser to Philippe. Edward refused to return Artois to France, and in response, Philippe declared Edward's Duchy of Aquitaine forfeit. With war looming, Edward revoked his homage for Aquitaine.

The issue of homage for Aquitaine should have been resolved by the Treaty of Brétigny of 1360 between Edward III and Jean II of France, following the English victory at Poitiers in 1356. Under a protocol associated with the Treaty, Edward III agreed to renounce his claim to the throne of France in return for French agreement that he should hold Aquitaine in full sovereignty. Unfortunately, for England, King Jean II (1350–1364) died in 1364 before these terms were put into effect, and the issue thus remained in the forefront of the quarrel between England and France. In 1369, Charles V reclaimed sovereignty over Aquitaine and Edward III took up the title of King of France again. In 1399, on his father's accession to the throne of England as Henry IV (1399–1413), the thirteen-year-old Prince Henry (the future Henry V, 1413–1422) was named Duke of Aquitaine. However, the dispute over sovereignty came into sharp focus again in early 1401 when the King of France, as a deliberate slight to Henry IV, named the Dauphin Louis, his eldest son as Duc de Guyenne (the French name for Aquitaine).

The importance of resolving the dispute over sovereignty for Aquitaine was not lost on the young Prince Henry, and it was a central tenet of his policy towards France after his accession as King Henry V in 1413.

The second cause of the war was the claim of English kings to the Crown of France. On the death of the French King Charles IV in 1328, the closest male successor was Edward III of England, through his mother Isabella, sister to Charles IV and daughter of his predecessor, Philippe IV.

The crux of the matter was whether the crown could be passed through the female line. The French view was that a woman could not inherit the crown and that she could not, therefore, pass this right to her son. Thus, Philippe, the next closest male successor, who could trace his lineage back to Philippe III through an unbroken male line, assumed the title of King Philippe VI – the first of the Valois dynasty. There was a somewhat desultory attempt by the English to lay claim to the throne on behalf of the fifteen-year-old Edward III. This received short shrift in France, and there the matter lay dormant until the third year of the war in 1340 when Edward formally claimed the Crown of France.

It is unclear whether Edward held this claim as a serious war aim. Since, in the Treaty of Brétigny, he was prepared to trade his claim to the throne for sovereignty over Aquitaine it may have been simply a way of encouraging allies and exerting negotiating pressure on Philippe VI, and on his successor Jean II. With the failure to implement the treaty, the issue remained unresolved throughout the rest of Edward III's life, and through the remainder of the war.

The Outbreak of War and the English Ascendancy, 1337–1360

First Moves

In May 1337, Philippe VI decided that the Duchy of Aquitaine should be forfeit because of Edward III's refusal to deliver Robert d'Artois into the hands of the French king. In response, Edward revoked his homage to Philippe. The French king had already proclaimed the *arrière-ban* to summon a royal army. The subsequent war, which was to span the reigns of five French and five English kings, and which is known to modern historians as the Hundred Year's War, had been unleashed.

At the start of the war, both kings expected that Aquitaine and the south-west of France would be the principal theatre of operations. Indeed, in the first years of the war there were some French incursions into Aquitaine, where a small number of English reinforcements had been despatched. There was also some cross-channel raiding by both sides, but as events unfolded, it became apparent to the English and to the French that the focus would be to the north – neither king went to the south-west.

THE BATTLE OF CASTILLON 1453

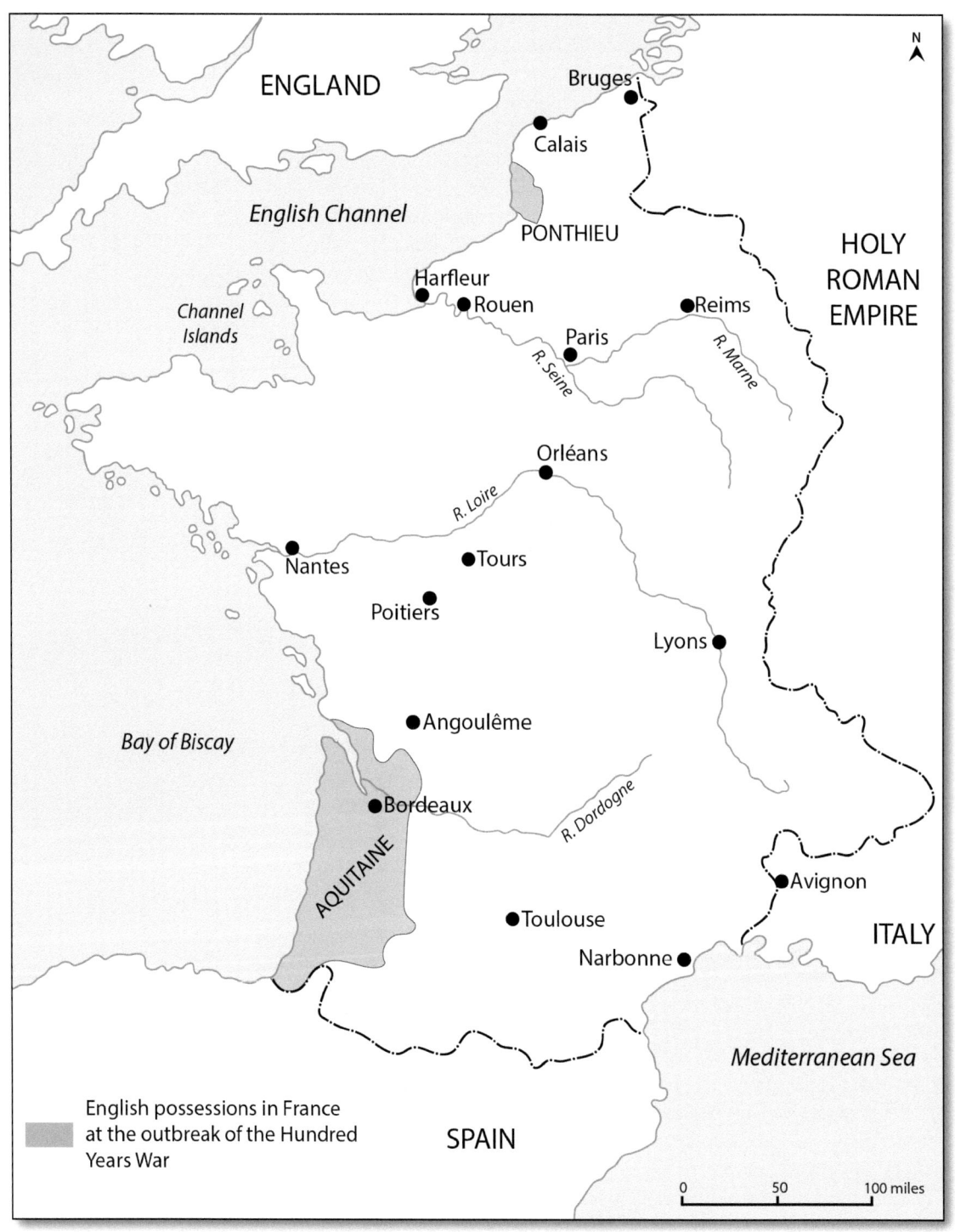

English Possessions in France 1337

With the focus on the north, attention turned to The Low Countries where there was widespread discontent with the relationship with France. Edward III sought to exploit the difficulties of Philippe by forging an alliance with Louis of Bavaria, the Emperor of the Holy Roman Empire (Louis IV, 1328–1346), and with discontented lords in The Low Countries. Edward landed at Antwerp in July 1338, and made his way to Coblenz. Here he was appointed the Emperor's Vicar, effectively vice-regent, in Western Europe for seven years and the Emperor's nobility gave Edward their homage. In July 1339, Edward summoned the nobles of the region to join his army, with the objective of recovering the area around Cambrai from France and restoring it to The Empire.

Edward's allies failed to arrive on time, and it was not until September that his army mustered. After a desultory attempt to take Cambrai by siege, the army moved into France and spread destruction in the hope of provoking Philippe to accept battle. However, by mid-October, the allied lords were becoming restless, and were on the point of dispersing to return home when the prospect of battle persuaded them to stay. The French and English armies assembled near the town of La Capelle, with Edward in a strong defensive position. In the event no battle took place and the French army melted away, and Edward's allies departed for home.

So far, Flanders had remained neutral, as the count had maintained a difficult balance between loyalty to the King of France and widespread internal opposition to his policy. However, Jacob van Artevelde, a powerful merchant from Ghent, had lent money to Edward and in return had secured the removal of restrictions on the import of English wool that was so important to Flanders. By late 1339, Artevelde had become the *de facto* ruler of Flanders and the count had fled to France. A problem for Edward and Artevelde was that if the Flemish fought for the King of England, they would be in breach of their allegiance to their overlord the King of France. The way around this problem was for Flanders to recognise Edward as King of France, and thus, in Ghent in January 1340, Edward formally proclaimed his claim to the French Crown.

English Successes in Flanders and Brittany – The Treaty of Malestroit

Edward returned to England to raise further subsidies, having expended huge sums during 1339 to pay and encourage his allies. In late June 1340, he set sail once again for Flanders, on the face of it this was a risky expedition. The French had had the upper hand at sea so far in the war, and a large fleet, including galleys furnished and crewed by the Genoese, had been assembled at Sluys in anticipation of Edward's return. Naval battles of the period were little different from combat ashore, with men boarding the enemy's ships to engage in hand-to-hand fighting. As on land, archers provided the English with a powerful weapon. The French chose to remain in harbour with ships chained together to await the English. In doing so, they sacrificed their ability to manoeuvre, while Edward's ships were free to do so and to optimise the use of their archers. The result was a crushing English victory in the first large-scale encounter of the war.

The success at Sluys brought in its train a treaty for Edward with Flanders, Hainault, and Brabant. The main objective for the coming campaign was to be Tournai, with the goal of bringing King Philippe to battle. The town was duly besieged while Philippe watched events from a distance. He failed to come to the relief of the town and after six weeks it seemed close to surrender. However, Edward was faced with problems holding his allies together and he had little option but to agree to a one-year truce, the Truce of Esplechin, to run from September 1340. Early the next year Edward's appointment as the Emperor's Vicar was withdrawn, and the alliance collapsed, ending two years of war with little to show for huge sums dispensed from the English exchequer.

In April 1341, the death of Jean III, Duke of Brittany, led to a disputed succession for the duchy between Jean de Montfort and Charles de Blois. Initially, the struggle was a sideshow. However, in early 1342 Edward III acceded to a request for help from Jeanne of Flanders on behalf of her husband Jean de Montfort, who was languishing in prison in Paris. An English force duly arrived in Brittany in May 1341, relieving the siege of Hennebout where Jeanne had taken refuge. A further English force, under the command of the Earl of Northampton, who had been appointed Edward's lieutenant in Brittany, arrived in Brest in July. Northampton advanced to Morlaix and, after an unsuccessful assault, settled down to besiege the town. Charles de Blois came to its relief in late September, and, in the first major land engagement of the war, the Earl of Northampton drove off the relieving force. More English troops were to follow into Brittany, with Edward arriving at Brest in person at the end of October 1342. The threat to France was now such that it drew in both King Philippe and his eldest son the Duke of Normandy, the future King Jean II. It looked in January 1343, as though there would be a set-piece battle between the French and the English, but once again, this was not to be. Later that month the intervention of the ambassadors of Pope Clement VI secured the Truce of Malestroit. The truce, which permitted the English and de Montfort's supporters to keep their gains, was intended to last three years – until September 1346.

A Return to War

During the next two years, there were frequent outbreaks of fighting, and finally, in June 1345, Edward renounced the truce.

With the resumption of war, Edward conceived a three-pronged attack on France: the Earl of Northampton from Brittany, the Earl of Derby in the south-west, and the King from Flanders. Edward crossed to Flanders, but his plans came to nothing following the assassination of Artevelde during a riot in Ghent in July 1345. However, the same month, the Earl of

Northampton, accompanied by Jean de Montfort, who had escaped from France the month before, returned to Brittany. The fighting continued through the winter and into 1346 with the English taking several towns, and in June 1346 Sir John Dagworth won a remarkable victory against superior numbers at Saint-Pol-de-Léon. Derby should have left for France at about the same time as Northampton left for Brittany, but he was delayed by the vagaries of weather in the Channel. He eventually landed in Bordeaux on 9 August 1345, and embarked on an aggressive campaign from the outset, capturing several key towns including Bergerac on the Dordogne, and La Réole and Aiguillon on the Garonne. In October 1345, he also defeated a substantially larger French army at Auberoche. The success of Derby drew the Duke of Normandy south; he elected to attempt to retake Aiguillon and settled down to besiege the town in April 1346.

The landing of Edward III in Normandy in July put Philippe VI in a difficult position. Jean, Duke of Normandy, was in the south-west with a substantial force facing a relatively minor threat, while the major challenge to the French developed in the north. The Duke of Normandy was recalled, but he was anxious to complete the siege before he departed. In the event he left for the north without taking the town, but he did not leave until 20 August, too late to be able to join his father's army at the Battle of Crécy.

The Crécy Campaign

While Northampton and Derby continued their operations during 1346, Edward revised his plans. Two further armies were now envisaged, one to be led by Edward III, and a further army drawn from his Flemish allies and led by Sir Hugh Hastings. The destination of Edward's army was announced as Gascony, with the assumed aim being to assist in raising the siege of Aiguillon. However, this was disinformation intended to confuse the French, and once the army was at sea, the true destination was revealed as Normandy. Godefroy d'Harcourt, a disaffected Norman noble in the service of Edward, may have proposed the landing in his ancestral lands of the Cotentin peninsular, but another factor may have been the historical link between England and the duchy through its possession by English kings in the twelfth century. Whatever the reason, Edward's fleet made landfall off Saint-Vaast on 12 July 1346. Edward's subsequent march through France culminated in the English victory at the Battle of Crécy, fought a little over six weeks later on 26 August 1346.

From Crécy to Brétigny

In the aftermath of Crécy, Derby kept the pressure on the French in the south-west and in September and October 1346 struck north as far as Poitiers, but the main theatre of operations remained the north. From Crécy-en-Ponthieu Edward III moved north with the objective of laying siege to Calais. On 4 September, the first English troops approached the town. Over the following 11 months, considerable resources and determination were required to bring the siege to a successful conclusion. Late in July 1347, Philip approached with a large army to relieve the town and issued a challenge to Edward. The English accepted the challenge but as so often in earlier years, the French army faded away. The last hope for the garrison and the inhabitants had gone and the town surrendered.

In September 1347, a further truce was agreed, to last initially until June of the following year. Although there was sporadic fighting in Brittany, the Calais Pale and Gascony during the formal respite in hostilities, the truce was extended several times until it finally collapsed in 1355. The focus now turned to Gascony, where the King of France's Lieutenant, the Count of Armagnac, was making worrying incursions into Aquitaine. Edward III despatched his eldest son Edward of Woodstock, Prince of Wales (later to become known as the Black Prince[2]), to Bordeaux, and between October and December 1355, he swept across the Languedoc as far as the Mediterranean before finally returning to Bordeaux. The following year, he moved north, and, at the Battle of Poitiers in September 1356, he won another great victory over the French. Poitiers was arguably the closest that the English came to winning a decisive battle during the Hundred Years' War, with the capture of the King of France, since 1350 Jean II, and France subsequently thrown into chaos. Jean II was taken to England in May 1357 and negotiations began to secure a lasting peace. It required a further English invasion, led by Edward III, in 1359 and 1360, marked by the unsuccessful siege of Reims, to finally force the French to agree terms. These were enshrined in the Treaty of Brétigny, which was ratified in Calais in October 1360.

The Peace of Brétigny

Under the Treaty of Brétigny, in addition to Edward III and Jean II trading sovereignty over Aquitaine for the English claim to the French Crown, huge tracts of South-West France were ceded to Edward. Thus, the first phase of war saw the English under Edward III in the ascendancy, but, due to the failure to implement all of its provisions, the Treaty of Brétigny, instead of providing the opportunity for a lasting peace, sowed the seeds for a renewal of war. On Jean's death in 1364, a substantial part of his ransom, agreed as part of the treaty, remained unpaid. The outstanding sum was to remain an issue between England and France, and its payment was an objective in Henry V's negotiations with the French 50 years later.

---

2   The soubriquet is an anachronism, but it is how Edward is most widely known today.

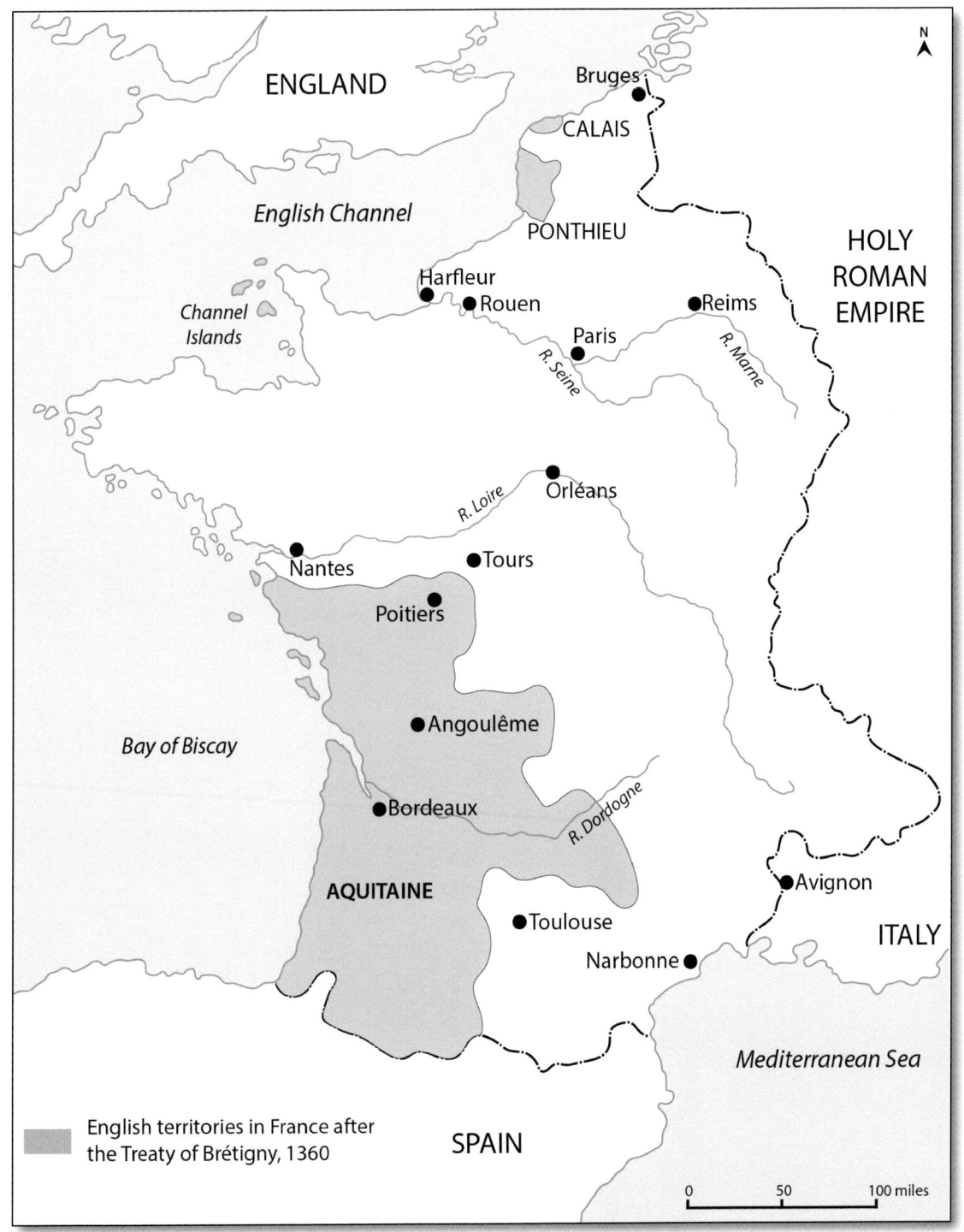

English Possessions After the Treaty of Brétigny 1360

The French Recovery, 1369–1389

Charles V succeeded Jean II as King of France in 1364. He had been a party to the Treaty of Brétigny, but since the joint renunciations, of sovereignty over Aquitaine by Jean and of his claim to the French Crown by Edward, had not been ratified Charles V refused to be bound by them. From Charles's accession, there was a steady deterioration in relations between France and England. In 1367, at Nájera in Spain, an Anglo-Gascon army commanded by the Black Prince, in support of Pedro the Cruel's claim to the throne of Castile, defeated the other claimant, Henry of Trastámara, and his Franco-Castilian army. Pedro reneged on his commitment to fund this campaign, and the Black Prince, who since 1363 had been prince of Aquitaine, had to resort to increased taxation on his subjects in Aquitaine to defray his costs. This resulted in considerable discontent, and in 1368 the Count of Armagnac, whose lands were within the newly expanded Aquitaine, appealed a dispute with the Black Prince to King Charles V. Charles was aware that hearing the appeal amounted to a rejection of English claims to sovereignty over Aquitaine, but nevertheless he issued a summons for the prince to appear in Paris in 1369. Unsurprisingly, the Prince failed to respond to the summons, and the war was renewed.

Charles V was too astute to repeat the experiences of his grandfather and father at the battles of Crécy and Poitiers, and avoided large-scale, set-piece battles. His strategy was to harass English armies and gradually push back the boundaries of English held territory by retaking towns and castles. The King was aided by a shrewd and effective commander, Bertrand du Guesclin, Constable of France, and by the time of Charles V's death in 1380, the English possessions had been reduced to the Calais Pale and a coastal strip near Bordeaux.

An Uneasy Truce, 1389–1415

The war continued, without either side making significant advances, until the Truce of Leulinghem in 1389. Negotiations to find a permanent peace dragged on but without success, and in 1396, to forestall the risk of a return to war, an extension to the truce was agreed. The truce was cemented by the marriage of King Richard II (1377–1399) to Isabella daughter of Charles VI (1380–1422). However, in 1399 Henry Bolingbroke, son of John of Gaunt, usurped the throne from his cousin Richard II to become King Henry IV. The French would not recognise Henry as the lawful King of England, but they did agree that the truce of 1396 would remain in force. Henry had his hands full at home both with rebellions and with trouble in Scotland and Wales, and the French, while stopping short of formally re-opening hostilities, missed no opportunity to create difficulties for the English with incursions into Aquitaine, support for the Scots, recognition of Owain Glyn Dŵr as Prince of Wales, and tacit support for acts of piracy against English shipping. From 1404 until early 1407 there were more determined, but unsuccessful, attempts to drive the English out of Aquitaine.

Within the French camp, Charles VI suffered from sporadic bouts of mental illness that, although never making him totally incapable of ruling, left a major weakness at the heart of French Government. This weakness was exacerbated by the struggle for power and feuding between Louis I, Duke of Orléans and his supporters (later known as the Armagnacs) and the Duke of Burgundy. Orléans, an erstwhile friend of Henry Bolingbroke while he had been in exile in France during the latter years of the reign of Richard II, turned violently against Henry after his usurpation of Richard's throne, and was the leading protagonist in attempts to drive the English from Aquitaine. The assassination of the Duke of Orléans in 1407 at the instigation of Jean the Fearless, Duke of Burgundy, relieved the pressure on the English in Aquitaine but also resulted in a period of political instability in France and complex diplomatic relationships for the rest of the reign of Henry IV.

A three-way relationship emerged between the Armagnacs, the Burgundians, and the English. Both French factions tried to gain English support as they manoeuvred for power, and the English attempted to exploit the weaknesses within France for their own ends. France descended into civil war during 1411 and 1412, with the English first intervening with an army led by the Earl of Arundel supporting the Duke of Burgundy and Charles VI against the rebel Armagnacs. In 1412, Henry IV, in response to a tempting offer from the Armagnacs that included recognition of English sovereignty over Aquitaine, sent an English army of 4,000 men commanded by the Duke of Clarence to support the Armagnacs. However, by the time, Clarence landed the rebels, Charles VI, and the Duke of Burgundy had come to terms and the competing factions were again at peace.

In March 1413, Henry V succeeded to the throne on the death of his father, Henry IV. Because of his father's usurpation of the throne and the history of rebellions during his reign, the new king could not feel entirely secure on his throne, but the situation in France was even more precarious. In early 1414, the Duke of Burgundy had fallen from power and been declared a traitor, and France once more descended into civil war with Charles VI, the Dauphin and the Armagnacs launching a war against the Duke of Burgundy. Meanwhile, Henry had agreed a ten-year truce with Jean V, Duke of Brittany, declaring the duke to be an ally.

Henry V had inherited from his father a campaign being waged in Aquitaine against the Armagnacs. This fighting came to a halt in early 1414, with a truce agreed to last for 12 months and applicable throughout France. Simultaneously, Henry was putting out feelers for a lasting peace, and offering terms, which included a marriage to Catherine de Valois, the daughter of Charles VI. With France in disarray from the internecine fighting, Henry felt emboldened enough by May 1414 to start to press his territorial claims on the French king. At about the same time, in parallel with his negotiations with Charles VI, he also started negotiating an alliance with the Duke of Burgundy to include mutual aid through the provision of men-at-arms and archers and a marriage to the duke's daughter. The Duke of Burgundy was prepared to help Henry conquer lands held by the Armagnac lords, but he would not go so far as to formalise an alliance against either Charles VI or the Dauphin.

The continuing part played by the initial causes of the war can be seen in Henry's demand for the restitution by Charles VI of lands granted under the Treaty of Brétigny, and the payment of the 1.6 million *écus* outstanding from the treaty for Jean II's ransom. He now went further, however: he demanded lordship over Normandy, Touraine, Maine and Anjou, the homage of Brittany and Flanders, and marriage to Charles's daughter Catherine, with a dowry of two million *écus*. Henry's hope was that, with the danger of an Anglo-Burgundian alliance hanging over them, Charles VI and his advisers could be pressurised into accepting these terms. The French were certainly concerned over the English negotiations with the Duke of Burgundy, but they were not prepared to go as far as Henry wanted. His ambassadors returned empty handed to England in October 1414.

A Return to War, 1415–1444

Meanwhile, Henry had begun to prepare for war. Parliament had agreed to grant taxes to support his policy, but it wanted Henry to continue to negotiate. In pursuit of a negotiated peace, the truce, due to expire in January 1415, had been extended until May, and English ambassadors crossed to France once more in February. By the time of the arrival of the English negotiators, Charles VI and the Duke of Burgundy had come to terms and agreed the Peace of Arras. The terms of the peace forbad any alliances with the English that could be prejudicial to the interests of the French Crown. Thus, when the negotiations reopened in March, Henry's ambassadors presented much-reduced territorial demands and progress was being made on the marriage between Henry and Catherine. The French, although their position had been much strengthened by the Duke of Burgundy's accommodation with the King, were ready to move some way towards Henry's demands over Aquitaine. However, they linked this concession to withdrawal of the English claim for the sum outstanding from Jean II's ransom. The English ambassadors withdrew from negotiations towards the end of March, declaring that they did not have the authority to agree the terms on offer. Henry had so far failed to exploit French divisions. However, he continued to try to come to an accord with the Duke of Burgundy during the spring and summer, and the French continued to harbour fears of an Anglo-Burgundian alliance. They also sought to delay Henry's preparation for war, and in June French ambassadors crossed to England. Negotiations, which were held with Henry in person, broke down acrimoniously and the ambassadors returned to France in early July.

As negotiations and preparations for war continued, Henry was acutely aware that his hold on the throne was insecure. There had been remarks by the French ambassadors that not only did he have no right to the French

THE HUNDRED YEARS' WAR

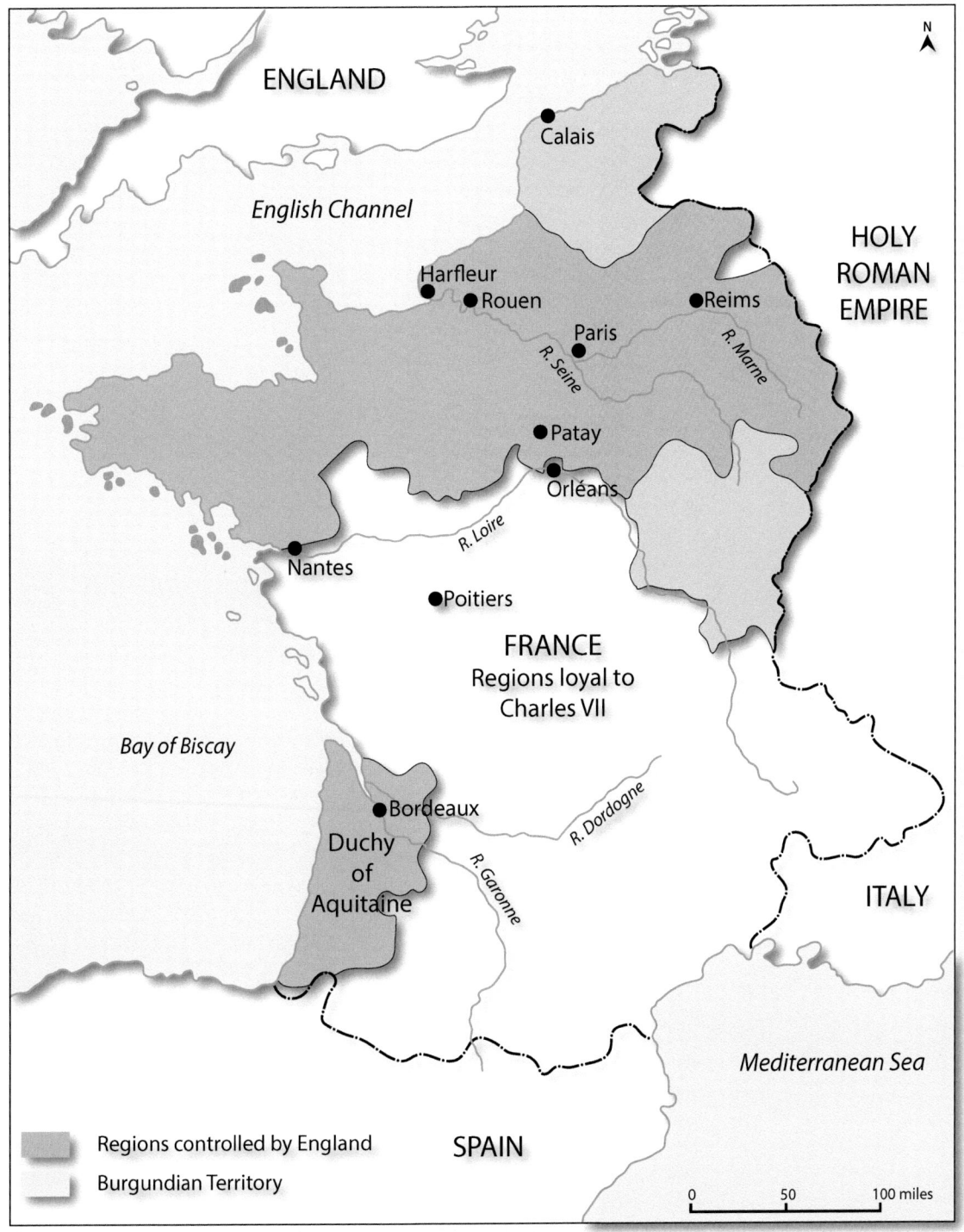

Anglo-Burgundian France in 1435

Crown but also that they should be negotiating with the true heirs of Richard II and not Henry, and there was apparently a plot against him on the eve of his departure from the Solent on 1 August 1415 (the Southampton Plot), which resulted in the summary execution of the Earl of Cambridge, Henry Lord Scrope, and Sir Thomas Grey.

Henry had intended to assemble an army for an expedition to France by 1 July but delays in mustering troops and gathering enough shipping delayed departure until 11 August. The landing was to be made in Normandy, probably with the objective of taking the duchy to strengthen Henry's bargaining position. Harfleur was the initial target, a useful bridgehead in northern France, which would also deny the French use of an important fortified naval base that had been used to launch attacks against the coast of England and English shipping. Having besieged and taken Harfleur, Henry marched northeast towards Calais and safety. On reaching the Somme, he found the ford at Blanchetaque near Abbeville, used by Edward III in 1346, too well defended by the French and he marched up-river until he was able to cross. He turned once again towards Calais, and confronted and defeated the French at Agincourt. After his victory, he continued to Calais and subsequently returned to England.

The Battle of Agincourt is popularly seen as the greatest English victory of the Middle Ages. However, despite the magnitude of the victory it was not decisive. Edward III, Henry's great grandfather, had been able to follow up his victory at Crécy with the siege and capture of Calais, and Edward III's son the Black Prince had captured Jean II at Poitiers, thus giving his father perhaps the closest that the English were to come to a decisive victory during the Hundred Years' War. After Agincourt, Charles VI remained at large, and Henry V did not have the means to follow up his victory that year. However, it did secure Henry's position on the English throne, and he could pursue his obsession with France unchallenged at home. He could now return to England, capitalise on his success, and plan for the future.

During August 1416, Sigismund of Luxembourg, King of the Romans (1410–1437, and subsequently Holy Roman Emperor 1433–1437), who had initially offered to mediate between the French and the English, recognised Henry's claim to the French Throne. In October 1416, Sigismund and Henry met the Duke of Burgundy at Calais. Henry was encouraged that, while Burgundy would not go so far as to recognise him as King of France, he would not stand in his way. Thus reassured, in August 1417 Henry set off again for France. His aim was to conquer the Duchy of Normandy and use it to enforce his claims, and now sieges of the major towns became the central element of Henry's strategy. By the end of September, Caen was in English hands. Other towns, including Bayeux, fell soon after and the conquest continued with Rouen, the greatest city of the duchy, falling in January 1419 after a siege of almost six months.

The Duke of Burgundy was meanwhile taking advantage of the English operations to launch attacks against the Armagnacs. However, there was ambiguity in the Burgundian position and there were occasions when English and Burgundian troops clashed. The French understood that their disunity was playing into the hands of Henry V, and attempts were made to resolve the differences between the factions. In September, the Duke of Burgundy met the Dauphin. Heated discussions ensued and Duke Jean was murdered by a member of the Dauphin's party, thus precipitating the very event that the Dauphin wished to avoid: pushing Burgundy, now ruled by the new duke, Philippe the Good, into the arms of the English. In December 1419, Henry and Philippe agreed to wage war together against the Dauphin. They also agreed that if Henry succeeded in his pursuit of his claim to the French Crown, the Duke of Burgundy would be his lieutenant for his French domains.

Henry now turned his attention to King Charles VI with negotiations that concluded with the Treaty of Troyes in May 1420. Under this treaty, Henry was to be the heir to Charles VI and to be Regent of France for the remainder of Charles's life. He was to retain the Duchy of Normandy by right of conquest and his entitlement to hold Aquitaine without homage was recognised. Little more than a week after the treaty was agreed Henry married Charles's daughter Catherine.

The Dauphin, who was by no means powerless, had, however, been consolidating his position. In response to his invoking the 'auld alliance' with Scotland a number of Scots had entered his service, and at Easter 1421 the Duke of Clarence was killed when he was defeated at Baugé by a Franco-Scottish Army. In June, Henry V returned to France. In December Henry's heir, the future Henry VI (1422–1461, first period) was born, but in August 1422, Henry V died of dysentery contracted during the siege of Meaux. Less than two months later Charles VI followed him to the grave. The infant Henry VI was proclaimed King of England and France.

Henry V's premature death at the age of 35 left his brother the Duke of Bedford as Regent in France. Under his Regency, there were further English victories, but the duke was faced with a range of problems as he struggled to build on Henry's legacy and consolidate English rule in France. He and the Duke of Burgundy controlled large areas of France, but outside of these areas, France was loyal to the Dauphin, and Bedford struggled to make further inroads into this territory. He also faced growing discontent from Henry VI's subjects in France, compelled to pay taxes to support the war, and a similar reluctance at home to pay for the continuing fighting. Difficulties with his allies compounded his problems. The Duke of Brittany moved back and forth between the French and English causes and the Duke of Burgundy was reluctant to pursue the war vigorously.

Then in 1429, Joan of Arc came onto the scene, bringing a change of fortune for the French. The English siege of Orléans was broken in May, and the retreating English army was defeated at the Battle of Patay the following month. The Dauphin, at Joan's urging, went to Reims and was crowned and anointed as Charles VII, giving a further boost to his standing and to French morale. The capture of Joan in 1430 and her subsequent trial and execution in 1431 offered the prospect of restored English fortunes, and the Duke of Bedford brought Henry VI to Paris to be crowned King of France in December. However, lack of funds from England to prosecute the war, and the continuing necessity of imposing taxes on the inhabitants of Normandy, led to increasing discontent among the population and an erosion of English control. The following year, the Duke of Burgundy was beginning to look for ways to break with the English. In 1435, the Duke of Bedford died, and only two weeks after his death Philippe the Good finally made peace with Charles VII in the Treaty of Arras.

The war continued with the French making inroads into English held lands. By 1444, the areas held by the English had been reduced to part of Aquitaine, the Calais Pale, the County of Maine, Lower Normandy, Harfleur (lost to the French in 1435 but recovered in 1440), and some other parts of Normandy. However, by now, both sides were ready for peace, and the Truce of Tours took effect on 1 June 1444. The truce was to run for 22 months, until 1 April 1446, but was extended initially for two years, until 1 April 1447, and then again until 1 June 1449 before finally collapsing in July 1449.[3]

---

3   Jean Chartier, *Chronique de Charles VII, Roi de* France (Vallet de Viriville ed.), (Paris: P Jannet, 1858), vol.2, pp.43 and 47–8.

2

The Military Reforms of Charles VII

The military reforms effected by Charles VII and developments in artillery were of fundamental importance to the defeat of the English after the breakdown of the Truce of Tours.

At the beginning of the Hundred Years' War French field armies were raised by the King through the *ban* and *arrière-ban*. The former was the mobilisation of the nobility and the latter called upon their vassals to rally to the Crown. This was essentially a feudal system, although knights, men-at-arms, and squires did receive wages. The system had several weaknesses: an absence of hierarchy and organisation, which resulted in a lack of discipline, fraud for payments to phantom soldiers and double counting of payments for horses, and freedom for men to leave the battle without dishonour if they did not like the turn of events. In addition, although this system could raise large numbers of men, many called to serve were poorly trained and badly equipped. There were also often, particularly for those raised by the *arrière-ban*, limitations to the service required; men could be called up for a limited period or restricted to serve in a limited geographical area.

The King was also dependent for money and men on the Estates (in effect the regional governments), and this could add further limitations. For example, after the Black Prince's *chevauchée* in the Languedoc in 1355, the Estates of Languedoc ruled that money raised for the war in 1356 would only be used in the defence of the Languedoc and would also be conditional upon the King sending his eldest son, the Dauphin and future Charles V, to lead the army. These feudal armies were, however, strengthened by the employment of mercenaries: often crossbowmen from the Italian city-states.

By contrast, Edward III had made major reforms to the raising of English armies. These were primarily raised by indenture; essentially contracts between the King and his nobles, who thus had a direct commitment to him. The nobles were contracted to raise specific numbers of men-at-arms and archers and were paid accordingly. The nobles in turn raised indentures with captains of lower rank. The result was that the English armies were better equipped and trained than those of the French. There was also a recognised hierarchy with nobles, captains and centenars and ventenars (responsible respectively for 100 and 20 men). In addition, because men often served the same captain for several campaigns, they were experienced and used to campaigning together. During Edward III's reign, men could also expect to make significant sums of money through the provisions in the indentures to share the spoils of war, often making a military career an attractive proposition.

After his accession to the French Throne in 1350, King Jean II set about making changes to the French system. The failures had been only too evident at Crécy, with an ill-disciplined attack on the English contrary to the wishes of Philippe VI (1328–1350). Jean II's reforms were limited but he had clearly recognised the need to make changes. Wages were increased and extended to archers, shield-bearers and infantry. Horses were to be marked and their descriptions recorded, and inspectors were appointed to audit muster rolls for both men and horses. Men-at-arms were required to select a captain, and companies were formed of between 15 and 80 men, with separate companies of infantry and archers. Captains of companies were required to serve under commanders of the divisions, normally the van, middle, and rear guards, and these in turn were subordinate to the Constable, the two Marshals and the Grand Master of Crossbowmen. Men could no longer leave the battle without permission of their captain and captains required the authority of their division commander before doing so.[1]

When Charles V succeeded Jean II in 1364, he continued with some further minor reforms. Notably, he encouraged competitions to improve the skills of archers and crossbowmen and raised taxes to fund a permanent army of around 5,000 men.[2] This army was initially organised in companies of 100 men to counter the Great Companies, bands of English and French brigands who had been wreaking havoc in France since the Treaty of Brétigny. To retain men, they were paid monthly, but to ensure that the taxes were well spent, wages were only disbursed after a satisfactory muster of men and equipment. These companies served Charles well for the purpose of defeating the Great Companies and taking their strongholds, and they proved to be a solid base in the resumption of war at the end of the 1360s.[3]

During the reign of Charles VI, France was plagued by civil war between the Armagnacs and the Burgundians. Not only were further reforms impossible, but also much that had been achieved by Jean II and Charles V fell by the wayside. It fell to Charles VII, once the nobles of France had been reconciled and set aside their internal quarrels, to embark on further reforms that contributed significantly to the change of French fortunes and the eventual defeat of the English at Castillon.

---

1 Jean Deviosse, *Jean le Bon* (Paris: Fayard, 1985), pp.190–5.
2 Jean Favier, *La Guerre de Cent Ans* (Paris: Fayard, 1981), p.321.
3 Françoise Arnaud, *Charles V, le Sage* (Paris: Fayard.1994), pp.602–4.

THE MILITARY REFORMS OF CHARLES VII

A catalyst for the reforms was the situation when the Truce of Tours was agreed in 1444. Charles VII found himself with large numbers of troops on his hands, and he was determined not to allow them to return to looting and ravaging the countryside. It is said that on the return of peace Charles VII asked one of his knights what he should do to control these men. The answer was to find them some useful employment elsewhere. This may have been apocryphal, but the ideal opportunity to do just that arose. The future Holy Roman Emperor Frederick III (1452–1493), since 1440 King of the Romans, and his cousin, Sigismund of Austria, were having great difficulty controlling part of the territory of The Empire in Switzerland. They had sought help from Burgundy but to no avail. During 1444, Frederick wrote to Charles VII asking for his help. With the English threat removed, at least for the time being, he could now send troops. The Dauphin, the future Louis XI, was despatched with a substantial army to support Frederick III against the Swiss Confederation. The English also contributed to this army with some 400 lances and a similar number of archers, although their detachment arrived too late to participate in the Battle of Saint Jakob an der Birs, near Basel, on 26 August 1444. The result of this battle was a crushing defeat for the Swiss. A treaty was concluded, and the French withdrew in early 1455. In doing so, they crossed Burgundy and Alsace. Ill-disciplined bands, much to the displeasure of Charles VII, engaged in looting and pillaging as they returned to France. Charles VII now needed once again to resolve the potential problem of bands of *routiers* causing havoc in France. He took the opportunity to embark on his reforms with the twin objectives of neutralising the companies of *routiers* and creating a more efficient army.[4]

The weakness of a system that relied on temporary armies raised for specific campaigns or sieges were evident to Charles VII. A successful siege was of little value if the enemy returned after the army had been demobilised. The answer was a standing army, and fortunately for the King he now had the means to sustain a substantial force. In 1445 and 1446 the King decreed that 15 companies, soon increased to 18, would be raised, each comprising 100 lances. Each lance was composed of six men: a man-at-arms, his page or valet, two mounted archers, and two grooms responsible for the six horses of the lance. The men were selected based on their age, height, strength, and the quality of their arms and horses. Only the most capable were accepted.[5] Thus, a considerable permanent force of between 7,000 and 8,000 men, if we discount some grooms who may not have been combatants, was potentially available to Charles VII. This force was known as the *Grande Ordonnance*; it provided the force for operations in the field. Although Charles VII was driven in large measure by the need to reform the army, he was also determined to put a stop to the pillaging of

---

4 Breuil, Jean de, (Léon Lecestre ed.), *Le Jouvencal*, vol.1 (Paris: Renouard, 1887), pp.xciii–v, cxii–cxv, cxx–cxxvii.
5 Thomas Basin, *Histoire de Charles VII et Louis XI*, (Paris: Éditions Pocket, 2018), p.201.

demobilised soldiers, which had become endemic in times of peace. As one chronicler recorded:

> … all the other pillagers, robbers, and wicked men, of which there were many, and who knew nothing and did nothing else than to destroy, rob and pillage his vassals and subjects, should be dispersed and prevented from committing these crimes, and thus it was ordered that within a few days all, under pain of capital punishment, must return from whence they came and return to work and follow their trades.[6]

Thus, other than the men who had been selected for the *Grande Ordonnance*, others under arms that were no longer required after the Truce of Tours were demobilised and ordered to return to their homes, or other places where they could find work, to cultivate the land or take up a trade.[7] The objective of this measure was not only to discourage redundant soldiers from forming into bands of brigands, as had often been the case in the past, but also to stimulate the recovery of agriculture and the economy. To ensure that the demobilisation was properly managed, commissioners were appointed to oversee the implementation of the King's decree. The demobilisation is reported as having been completed in the remarkably short period of 15 days.[8]

After so many years of war, towns and countryside were impoverished and the tax raising capacity was much reduced. To reduce the burden on the Crown the *Grande Ordonnance* was dispersed across the country in units of around one hundred lances, with responsibility placed on the various places to equip and sustain the companies. These units were themselves often dispersed in turn, with as small a unit as a single lance being lodged with a parish or a group of parishes. In view of the economic situation, it was often impossible to raise sufficient money to pay the costs in full and part would often be paid in kind, in the form of food for men and horses. As the economic situation improved, and tax revenue started to flow once again, the Crown took back the responsibility for the payment of wages to the lances.[9]

However, to address the problem of holding towns or fortresses retaken from the English the field army was supplemented by the *Petite Ordonnance*. By 1451 there were 550 men-at-arms, each with two archers and a page, assigned to this force, adding more than 2,000 men to the standing royal army.

---

6   Monstrelet, Enguerrand de, *Chroniques*, Ed. J. A. Buchon, vol.10 (Paris: Verdière, 1826), p.44.
7   Basin, *Histoire de Charles VII et Louis XI*, p.202.
8   Breuil, *Le Jouvencal*, vol.1, p.cxxviii, n.2.
9   Basin, *Histoire de Charles VII et Louis XI*, pp.202–3.

THE MILITARY REFORMS OF CHARLES VII

However, this was not the whole story, and the King could still raise men for specified periods and campaigns. For the reconquest of Gascony from 1451 onwards, it has been estimated that the French could put more than 20,000 men in the field, with a further 3,000 assigned to hold the towns and fortresses taken from the Anglo-Gascons.

The next step in the reforms was the creation in 1448 of the *franc-archers* – literally 'free archers', 'free' because they were exempted from taxes. A wage of four francs per month was paid, but only if the men were called to royal service away from their home parish.[10] Each parish was required to contribute one man, either an archer or crossbowman, per 80 households, and to maintain his equipment. In theory this would raise a permanent reserve of a further 8,000 infantry. Also in theory, those selected as *franc-archers* were supposed to be fit, strong and experienced. In reality the system did not incentivise young men whose resources were insufficient to attract taxation, but rather notables who were more attracted by the financial advantages than military service. Thus, many of those who enlisted were the sick, the infirm and the old. Others enjoyed the companionship of their fellows in the local tavern rather than on the training ground. The institution survived little more than 30 years and was abolished in 1480 by Louis XI.[11] The mediocre military value of the *franc-archers* was appreciated at the time, and they were frequently relegated to secondary roles in support of the artillery, as field engineers to prepare artillery positions, and as escorts for the artillery train when on campaign.[12] While all these reforms were in progress the English system stood still, rooted in the innovations of Edward III. The increasing difficulties for the English of raising money for their armies, coupled with the developing quarrels between the Houses of Lancaster and York meant that the English were at a significant disadvantage when war broke out again in 1449.

---

10 Breuil, *Le Jouvencal*, vol.1, p.cxxvii, n. 3.
11 Favier, *La Guerre de Cent Ans*, pp.588–91, Basin, *Histoire de Charles VII et Louis XI*, pp.203–4.
12 H. Dubled, 'L'Artillerie Royale Française à l'Époque de Charles VII au Début du Règne de Louis XI (1437–1469) Les Frères Bureau', *Sciences et Techniques de l'Armement, Mémorial de l'Artillerie Française*, 50:4 (1976), p.586.

3

Evolution in Artillery During the Hundred Years' War

Overview

Gunpowder artillery first made its appearance in Europe in the early fourteenth century. It was present with the English army of Edward III at the Battle of Crécy in 1346, but it appears that it was more notable for its dramatic effect of smoke and noise than for its efficacy as a weapon. A century later the place of artillery in warfare had changed dramatically, both because of the deployment of guns in much greater numbers and of technological developments. In the early years of the war, mechanical stone-throwing machines remained predominant for siege warfare and defence of towns and fortresses. However, as the war progressed cannon became more effective, and increasingly more common. By the mid-fifteenth century it had become necessary to modify the design of fortifications to counter increasingly effective artillery. By around 1430, the first man-portable guns were making their appearance, but the use of gunpowder weapons on the battlefield remained limited throughout the Hundred Years' War – until the Battle of Castillon.

The Early Years

The earliest cannon were generally small, often weighing little more than 30lbs and rarely exceeding 100lbs. The projectiles of early cannon usually resembled large crossbow bolts rather than balls, much as those fired from springalds or ballista (large forms of crossbows usually used in static defence). However, there is some evidence of early weapons being used to fire solid lead balls and incendiary projectiles in the form of red-hot iron balls. Problems with early cannon were numerous: the high cost of both guns and powder, the difficulty of achieving quality, short barrel life, and maintaining gas pressure on firing the powder due to gas leaks from the gun structure and around the projectile.

The Middle Years, c.1375 to c.1430

By the mid–1370s stone cannon balls were making their appearance and cannon were becoming larger, now weighing up to 2,000lbs. These large calibre weapons, generally known as bombards, were intended for attacks on walls and fortifications. They were capable of firing balls weighing up to 300lbs, and were beginning to compete with mechanical stone-throwing machines for effectiveness. Some problems remained however. Powder was fine and if it were compressed during loading it was difficult to achieve rapid and uniform combustion, which resulted in a loss of power. To maximise the explosive force, it was necessary to avoid packing the gunpowder too tightly, and to leave a space between the powder and the projectile for efficient combustion. This was achieved by inserting a soft wooden wad between the powder and the ball – it was the propulsion of the wad that propelled the ball rather than the explosion itself. However, stone balls were frequently smaller in diameter than the barrel and/or of irregular size, and thus did not fit tightly in the bore. To achieve maximum power from the propulsion it was important that the ball was loaded tight up against the wad – this was achieved using small wooden wedges to hold the ball in position.

An early cannon, c.1380; note the removable powder chamber with a narrower calibre than the barrel, held in place with a wooden wedge to minimise gas loss around the joint. (Alain Parbeau)

A further development during this period was the manufacture of smaller bore cannon, firing balls of between 3lbs and 20lbs. These smaller weapons were often mounted on wooden frames, which were sometimes wheeled. One form of smaller cannon was known as the veuglaire, which started to make its appearance from late in the fourteenth century and into the first quarter of the fifteenth century. These weapons were initially of Flemish or German origin. Smaller calibre guns were primarily intended for use against personnel, both from within fortified places or in battle. They usually had a removable powder chamber. They were generally relatively light in weight, typically between 60lbs and 200lbs, although larger pieces up to 1,000lbs also existed. The veuglaires also typically had longer barrels than earlier cannon. This feature, combined with the development of more precisely manufactured balls to provide a better fit to the barrel, and better quality powder resulted in a higher muzzle velocity, and improved accuracy.

With these developments in cannon, gunpowder artillery began to take precedence over mechanical machines for siege warfare. They were used in three modes: high elevation fire to reach over walls, direct fire against walls and fortifications, and (with longer barrels and better fitting balls) precision fire against specific targets. At the same time cannon were deployed in towns and fortresses for defensive purposes. Larger guns were used for counterbattery fire, leading to the development of wooden shelters for siege guns, while smaller guns were deployed for anti-personnel use. The evolution of heavier cannon also led to developments in fortifications to reduce the effectiveness of direct fire and to provide embrasures and emplacements for cannon.

The Final Phases of the Hundred Years' War

Around the time of the siege of Orléans of 1428–9, a new form of weapon appeared, the culverin (the name derives from the French word, *cuivre*, for copper, although they were often fabricated in bronze or iron). Culverins ranged from small calibre portable weapons weighing from 15 to 20lbs to heavier weapons of 100lbs in weight. These weapons were characterised by several technical innovations. All fired lead balls, which could be manufactured with precision, thus ensuring a good fit to minimise leakage of gas from the combustion of the powder. With less leakage, wads were no longer required. The removable powder chambers were dispensed with. Charging with powder was by means of a funnel and rod. The acceleration of the ball was achieved by longer barrels, as distinct from the propulsion by the wad in earlier weapons. The improved acceleration was also achieved due to the development of high-quality granular powder, which improved consistency, and speed of combustion.

A reproduction cannon representative of French artillery during the mid-fifteenth century (Alain Parbeau)

An important development during this period was the reduction in unit cost of handguns, with greater numbers of weapons being produced. Even with the cost of lead balls and better quality powder the cost of each shot was roughly equivalent to that of a crossbow. By around 1430 the cost of manufacture of a handgun was less than half that of a crossbow. Furthermore, the time to train a handgunner was similar to that for a crossbowman and, additionally, the former did not require the strength and specialist skills of a longbow archer.

In addition to the appearance of the lighter culverins was the production of much heavier bombards. A famous example is Mons Meg in Edinburgh Castle. Built in 1449, this gun weighed six tons, had a barrel length of more than 13 feet, a calibre of 18 inches and could fire a ball weighing up to 330lbs. The problem with these large

Reproduction culverin handgun c.1410 (Alain Parbeau)

EVOLUTION IN ARTILLERY DURING THE HUNDRED YEARS' WAR

A replica bombard at Tiffauges Castle in France. Note the movable wooden shield to protect gunners during reloading. (Peter Hoskins)

weapons was that elevated fire to cross walls was not easy to achieve and they were limited to direct fire. To cross walls mortars were developed with short barrels allowing easy elevation. These heavier guns also required considerable numbers of horses or oxen for their deployment.

Despite these considerable developments the use of gunpowder artillery on the battlefield remained strictly limited. This can be attributed to the weight and lack of manoeuvrability of large pieces, the slowness of reloading and the vulnerability of gunners, and to the fact that hand-held weapons were still available only in relatively small numbers. Artillery was to have a decisive role at Castillon, but this was largely due to the use of guns in a strong defensive position.

Powder

The basic mix of gunpowder, of charcoal, sulphur, and saltpetre remained unchanged as technology developed, although various experiments were made with additional substances in the hope of increasing the explosive power. However, with time, different grades of powder were introduced: a coarser powder for large cannon, a finer mix for medium calibre weapons and a finely ground powder for portable weapons. Additionally, a very finely ground powder was used for ignition of the main charge for larger cannon. By around 1430, a granulated powder was coming into use. This powder was more powerful for a given weight than ground powder. However, barrels deteriorated more rapidly, and use of granulated powder only became widespread with the introduction of stronger, bronze cannon. The key characteristic of granulated powder was that it burnt faster than ground powder, thus imparting maximum power before the ball left the barrel. In parallel with the development of varieties of powder came a greater sophistication in determination of the size of the charge of powder. During the fifteenth century, the quantity of powder was calculated according to the strength of the piece, the weight of the projectile, the calibre of the barrel, and the distance to, and the nature of, the target.

Innovations

Other innovations in this period greatly improved the efficiency of cannon. Among these were the refinement of gun carriages and the introduction of trunnions. The role of the bombard was as a siege weapon to fire a projectile against defended towns or fortresses. Thus, mobility was not an important criterion, and the carriages were fixed. Nevertheless, it was necessary to be able to change the orientation of the carriage and the elevation of the barrel to aim at the target. A wooden chassis that could be rotated came into use and the elevation could be adjusted with a simple system of levers. For smaller calibre weapons wheeled carriages were introduced. Initially, these carriages had four small wheels, and this remained the case for weapons such as mortars. However, for other pieces carriages with two large wheels appeared during the fifteenth century. Initially, the trail for the gun was a single piece that supported the barrel. The orientation of the gun could be easily changed with the wheeled carriage, but adjustment to the elevation required a ratchet system. A weakness with this design was that with the barrel supported on a single trail the change of elevation was limited. It is not clear where the innovation first appeared, but in France the Bureau brothers adopted the split trail, where the barrel could be elevated between the two arms of the trail, thus significantly increasing the degree of change of elevation that was possible. The introduction of trunnions provided a further refinement and for the first time the elevation of the barrel could be altered easily to adjust the aim of the cannon.

The development of granulated powder meant that a greater explosive force was produced more quickly. This resulted in smaller calibre, but longer barrelled, weapons to maximise the effectiveness of the propulsion to give higher muzzle velocity, greater range, and better impact velocity.

A *veuglaire*. The removable powder chamber and mechanism for adjusting elevation are visible at the rear of the piece. (Nicolas Savy)

Terminology and New Types of Gun

Terminology for different types of guns is imprecise and can be confusing. Broadly speaking, from the 1430s, in addition to the bombards and veuglaires already in use, new weapons began to appear, culverins, crapaudins, and serpentines. These all had the common feature of longer barrels and smaller calibres than earlier guns and, in principle, the culverin was a portable handgun with the crapaudin and serpentine being progressively larger guns. However, there was no hard and fast specification, and some culverins were far too heavy to be used as portable weapons. Nevertheless, with the culverin the first practicable portable guns appeared, and they were used by the French as early as 1429 at the siege of Orléans. Culverins took time to reload, which rendered the user vulnerable between shots – a disadvantage that they shared with crossbows. Nevertheless, they were to play an important part at Castillon in 1453.

Improvements to Projectiles

In the earliest days of gunpowder artillery, the natural tendency was to use similar projectiles to those used in mechanical artillery: large bolts, similar to those used in crossbows, pieces of wood with an iron cap, and roughly hewn balls of stone. However, badly finished stone cannon balls quickly damaged barrels and better made balls soon started to become predominant. A drawback of stone cannon balls was that they lacked solidity for use against stone walls, particularly if the projectile was of a softer stone than the target. Around the time of the Bureau brothers this weakness was countered by encircling the ball with an iron hoop. Another metal that was used was lead and this became usual for the projectiles of hand-held weapons. Lead had the advantage of being easy to work with, but it was soft; while this was not a great problem for small calibre anti-personnel weapons, it was a significant disadvantage when firing against stone walls. A compromise was reached to exploit the malleability of lead to give a smooth surface to the ball, but, to retain the penetrative power of forged iron, cannonballs were made from roughly shaped iron balls with a smooth lead case. However, both lead and the process were prohibitively expensive. The breakthrough came with the development of the ability to manufacture cast iron balls.

The cast iron cannonball had advantages over earlier projectiles. First and foremost, it was much more effective against walls, but furthermore, it was easier to manufacture with consistent precision and thus was a better fit to the barrel. The consequence of this was that there was less escape of gas during firing and the muzzle velocity was higher, and thus for a given effect, less powder was required. With stone firing bombards effectiveness relied on a high trajectory and a large explosive charge.

With the new technology lighter cannon were produced which used much less powder for a given effect. In addition, whereas in the past a bombard required a high plunging trajectory to inflict damage, the new lighter cannon could achieve good results with a flatter trajectory. With these changes came smaller calibres and lighter, more powerful, and more mobile cannon. The effective range of cannon was now in the order of 1,000 metres, and when used in the field in sufficient quantity, as was the case at Castillon, this to some extent negated the legendary advantage of the English longbow – with the enemy engaged before they came within bowshot.

With the cast iron ball came other innovations for anti-personnel use: balls cut into four pieces attached by two chains joined in the middle, and two discs of iron attached by a chain. Cannonballs were also heated to red-hot temperature to be used as incendiary devices. One weapon developed for anti-personnel use on the battlefield was the ribaudequi*n* – a multi-barrel weapon firing small calibre balls. Nevertheless, despite these developments the continued poor mobility of heavy guns and lengthy time needed to reload, and the vulnerability of gunners meant that gunpowder artillery was still not widely used on the battlefield and was largely employed in static defensive or siege deployment.[1]

A ribaudequin multi-barrel anti-personnel weapon. (Nicolas Savy)

The Bureau Brothers

The development of artillery was more evolutionary than revolutionary, and it is impossible to date many of the innovations with any certainty, or indeed to attribute them to any given person. Nevertheless, the French were in the forefront in exploiting technological developments and making administrative and tactical innovations to optimise the use of artillery. Consequently, artillery was a key factor in the rapid reconquest of the English held territory in the Île-de-France (1437–1441), Normandy (1449–50) and Gascony (1450–1453). Much of the credit has traditionally been

---

1   Emmanuel Crouy-Chanel, *Canons Médiévaux, Puissance du feu* (Paris: Rempart, 2010), gives a detailed analysis of the development of gunpowder weapons in the Middle Ages.

given to two brothers: Jean and Gaspard Bureau, who had an important role to play in the exploitation of the more capable weapons that were being developed.

The Bureau brothers came from a bourgeois family but through their talents rose to take positions of high rank in French society. They were the primary architects of artillery as a distinct component of French armies as opposed to an auxiliary arm subordinate in administration and employment to the infantry and cavalry.

Jean Bureau, born in Paris between 1387 and 1393, had ambitions for a military life, but displayed a talent for administration. Between 1425 and 1435, he held a senior position in the administration of Paris during the English occupation, but he passed into the service of Charles VII on the departure of the English in 1436, becoming a counsellor of the King the following year. In 1440, he became Treasurer for the Kingdom of France. In 1443, he took on a further post, in effect chairman of the committee overseeing royal finances, and was thus in the unusual position of supervising his other role as treasurer. He was now in a powerful position to pursue his conviction that the artillery must be developed methodically. He was held in high regard by the King, and was frequently employed on diplomatic missions. Jean also pursued his military ambitions exploiting the growing importance of artillery by taking part in operations from 1437 with the siege of Montreau, through to beyond the end of the Hundred Years' War. He died in Paris in 1463, 10 years after the end of the war, having continued in service with the new King Louis XI.

Gaspard, the third of three Bureau brothers, was probably around six years younger than Jean, having been born between 1393 and 1400. To posterity he is somewhat in the shadow of his elder brother, but it was Gaspard who was the technician able to put their ideas into practice. Gaspard, like his brother, started his service as a financial administrator but moved on to a military career. In 1441, he became acting Master of Artillery and was confirmed in post in 1444 on the resignation of the incumbent through ill health. As with his brother he continued into the service of Louis XI until his death in 1469.

Changes and Developments During the Time of the Bureau Brothers

Although the Bureau brothers are credited with much of the progress made with artillery in French armies during the fifteenth century a note of caution is necessary since it is not entirely clear how much direct involvement the brothers had in specific developments. Nevertheless, it can be safely said that through their administration of the new arm, the exploitation of new manufacturing capacity, technical innovation, and the employment of artillery in warfare they were of fundamental importance in bringing the war to a successful conclusion for France.[2]

Organisation

In the early years of gunpowder artillery in French armies the organisation of the arm was haphazard and often ad hoc. The artillery was subordinate to either the Marshals or the Grand Master of Crossbowmen, and when officers were appointed to command artillery, it was usually for a specific campaign. Within towns where artillery was held, officers would also be appointed, but there was no overall coherent structure for the control and employment of this new arm. Much as many of the French nobility held infantry and archers in contempt, they also showed great disdain for artillery, and the officers for the artillery, as with the Bureau brothers, were drawn from men of lower rank. The advantage was that these men were often more open minded and more favourable to innovation than were members of the nobility.

It was only much later that the Master of Artillery became a grand master on a par with other senior officers of the Crown. Nevertheless, from 1437 the office of Master of Artillery became permanent, albeit subordinate to the Grand Master of Crossbowmen. With Gaspard Bureau's appointment, initially in an acting capacity, the responsibilities of the Master of Artillery became more clearly defined and broader in scope. He had command of the artillery on campaign but also considerable financial and administrative responsibilities. He was required to prepare an annual budget for the artillery, including for repair of existing pieces and procurement of new cannon. He had to account to the King for the expenses associated with sieges and, each month, for expenses of the artillery. He was responsible to the royal chamber of accounts and employed inspectors to supervise artillery held in the royal arsenals and fortresses.

Manufacture

In the early days of gunpowder artillery, the manufacture of cannon was in the hands of individual artisans and there was no consistency in design or calibre. Early cannon were manufactured from strips of forged iron, constructed much as barrels with the strips held together by iron hoops. Rust and defects in the welding between strips resulted in short barrel life for such cannon. The powder for early cannon was supplied by means of a removable breech chamber attached to the barrel while the projectile was

---

2   For a detailed discussion of the development of artillery in the time of the Bureau brothers see Dubled, 'L'Artillerie Royale Française à l'Epoque de Charles VII at au Début du Règne de Louis XI (1437–1469) Les Frères Bureau', pp.555–637.

muzzle loaded. These breech chambers were ill fitting with the result that gas escaped, to the detriment of the propulsive force of the explosion and also constituting a danger to the gunners. There was a further problem: the chambers were held in place by a form of calliper or bracket, which, due to the recoil of the cannon, again had a short life and could sometimes become detached and constitute a further danger for those serving the piece.

At about the time that the Bureau brothers were beginning to have an influence on artillery important changes in manufacture were starting to occur. First, techniques for casting cannon began to be developed, initially with smaller calibre weapons but in due course also for heavier guns. Cast cannon were easier to manufacture and repair, although the casting process was dangerous, and had a longer life than forged guns. As casting techniques developed, a further important innovation was the use of metals other than iron. Copper was initially used but quickly gave way to bronze; in the fifteenth century an alloy of approximately 90 percent copper and 10 percent tin. Bronze had the advantage of being stronger and more reliable than copper and forged and cast iron. The downside was that it was expensive.

While manufacture was largely undertaken by small, independent artisans few were ready to take the risk of investing in bronze, beyond small numbers of weapons of small calibre. However, several factors resulted in the widespread adoption of bronze: the arrival of the Bureau brothers on the scene with their commitment to improving artillery, the improved financial situation of Charles VII, and, thanks to a number of powerful merchants, thriving commerce for France in the fifteenth century, which encouraged investment in manufacturing. With his appointment as Master of Artillery, Gaspard Bureau was able to capitalise on these changes and carry forward his vision for artillery, including the widespread use of bronze. Foundries began to multiply in the towns, many based on bell foundries, which took on the production and repair of cannon. In 1450 a further office was created to oversee the production of arms throughout the realm.

From the time of the Bureau brothers, there was a further innovation to overcome the problems caused by the system of charging cannon with a removable breech block: the casting of the cannon in a single piece and the charging of the weapon by the muzzle. This resulted in greater efficiency and reduced the risks for the gunners. Initially this change was limited to the larger calibre guns because of the greater explosive power involved, but it was subsequently adopted for all calibres. Muzzle-loading weapons were to remain in service for four centuries until the arrival of steel cannon with movable gas-tight breech blocks in the later nineteenth century.

Administration

Before gunpowder artillery became predominant, mechanical siege artillery was often constructed on site. This was clearly not possible with cannon, and they needed to be deployed with the army. They required considerable resources to move them and to support them in the field with powder and projectiles. They absorbed a good deal of manpower and horses or oxen. Cannon brought from England had played a significant part in Henry V's successful siege of Harfleur in 1415. However, when he left for his march to Calais, which was to culminate in the Battle of Agincourt, he left his artillery behind – presumably because he saw it as more of an encumbrance than an advantage. With lighter more mobile artillery deployed in greater numbers good logistical support was required. Under the Bureau brothers the concept of the artillery park was born. In effect, for a given campaign the artillery and all that was needed to support it was centralised. If the main force were split, then resources would be allocated to each element, but the park would remain centralised. During sieges gun batteries would, of necessity, be deployed forward to within effective range of the defences, but the park, sometimes connected to the batteries by communication trenches, would be kept out of range of defensive cannon. The park would normally be surrounded by trenches and palisades and defended by the *franc-archers*.

As mentioned, from 1437 the post of Master of Artillery, although still subordinate to the Grand Master of Crossbowmen, had wide ranging financial and administrative responsibilities for the artillery of the French armies. Below the Master of Artillery there were deputies, known as *commis*, appointed either by the King or by the master, with responsibility for the artillery for the duration of particular campaigns or sieges. Jean Bureau was appointed to the post for several sieges and campaigns in Normandy and Gascony. As early as 1411 the craftsmen who manufactured cannon were required to have a recognised qualification and were organised in corporations (a body similar in function to English guilds). They were known as master gunners. Not only were they responsible for the manufacture of the cannon, but they were also required to serve the pieces in time of war. Within the hierarchy they were subordinate to the *commis*. An important innovation by the Bureau brothers was the employment of the *franc-archers* after their creation in 1448. Their mediocre value as combatants was quickly recognised but they were a useful labour resource. They were employed in support of the artillery as general labourers, field engineers and sappers to construct trenches, defences, and mines. They also served as escorts for the artillery on the march and to defend the artillery parks.

Employment

In February 1429, during the siege of Orléans, a French raiding party attacked an English supply column at Rouvray-Saint-Denis, a battle that has gone down in history as the Battle of the Herrings because the provisions included barrels of salted herrings in preparation for Lent. The English force, under the command of Sir John Fastolf, was attacked by a numerically superior Franco-Scottish force. The English had time to form their wagons into a defensive formation and the archers to drive stakes into the ground to hamper the French cavalry. In the opening stages of the battle the French made effective use of artillery firing from beyond the range of the English archers, inflicting casualties and damaging wagons. However, an ill coordinated attack by the Scots forced the French to stop their artillery fire for fear of inflicting casualties on their allies. The result was that the English men-at-arms and archers prevailed in the time-honoured way. Nevertheless, the first signs of the potential of modern artillery skilfully used were apparent. A few months later, in June 1429, the growing potential for artillery on the battlefield was demonstrated at the Battle of Patay, where artillery fire pressurised the English men-at-arms to attack the French positions. Although the effectiveness of artillery in pitched battle was becoming more important, the inherent disadvantages remained. The advantages flowing from the developments of artillery were initially most evident in attacks on towns and fortresses. Lengthy sieges were no longer the order of the day as walls and defences quickly succumbed to modern artillery. It was the effectiveness of artillery in sieges that was instrumental in the rapid conquest by the French of the English held towns and castles when war resumed in 1449.

4

An Uneasy Peace, The Truce of Tours 1444–49

When the Truce of Tours was signed in May 1444 there was relief and rejoicing in both countries. The truce gave the people of Normandy and the French domains of Charles VII the chance to rebuild towns and villages and recultivate land that had been neglected because of the war. Trade blossomed within and between the lands held by the English and the French. There were hopes in both France and England that a permanent peace could be found during the two years of the truce. Among the Normans in particular the coming of peace gave rise to hopes of seeing the French King regaining control of Normandy, to allow normal life to resume particularly for those with relations in the rest of France.[1] The Truce was extended several times before finally collapsing in July 1449, a collapse that was followed by the rapid conquest by Charles VII, in little more than a year, of all the remaining English held territory in northern France except the Calais Pale which remained in English hands until 1558. In the autumn of 1450, France turned its attention to Aquitaine, resulting in the defeat of Shrewsbury's army at Castillon and the English finally being driven from South-Western France in 1453. After so many years of war, the complete expulsion of the English from Aquitaine was achieved in a little over four years.

The seeds of this turnaround in fortune lay in the different conduct of the English in France and at home during the five years of truce. In England there were high hopes that a peace settlement could be reached; indeed, Henry VI seems to have been convinced that it was possible. On the French side Charles VII, although probably willing to agree peace if the right terms could be found, seems to have viewed the uneasy peace of the truce as a time to recover from the exhaustion of the years of war and to prepare for a return to hostilities when the time was right.

---

1   Monstrelet, *Chroniques*, vol.10, pp.5–9.

AN UNEASY PEACE, THE TRUCE OF TOURS 1444-49

The difficulty with negotiating a peace centred, as it had done for many years, on the question of sovereignty: Henry VI was prepared to renounce his claim to the French Crown but in return he wanted full sovereignty over English possessions in Normandy and Aquitaine, but this Charles would not, and could not, concede. Senior delegations were sent from both realms, led by the Archbishop of Rheims for the French and the Duke of Suffolk for the English, to try to negotiate terms but neither side would compromise and there was thus no progress.[2] A problem for Henry VI was that any concessions over English held territory, which might help in negotiations with Charles, would alienate English landowners who held property in France. A case in point was the County of Maine, centred on Le Mans, which Henry VI, initially secretly, offered to cede to René, Duke of Anjou, and his brother Charles, Duke of Maine. The Duke of Anjou was the father of Henry's new bride and Queen, Margaret of Anjou, and there may have been a case for Maine coming to Henry VI as part of her dowry. The problem was that Charles VII would not countenance that. The unconditional transfer of the county was perhaps a reflection of Henry's naivety. He clearly thought that Charles VII shared his desire for peace at all costs and probably saw his offer as a mark of good faith. The objective may have been to persuade the two brothers to support the English case for peace. Unfortunately, this support did not materialise, unsurprisingly since the offer was unconditional and when the county was given up in 1448 there was no *quid pro quo* from the French and hence no incentive for the Dukes of Anjou and Maine to intervene in Henry's interest.

This concession became a thorn in the side for Henry. When the news became public there was consternation not only among the English landowners in the county but also in England in Parliament. Compensation was promised but despite protracted negotiations this did not materialise. However, it was not only a problem at home for Henry but also in France. English officials and captains employed a variety of subterfuges to attempt at best to stop the transfer, or at least to delay it. Consequently, the transfer dragged on and gave rise to numerous incidents that gave Charles VII grounds for complaints about the lack of observance of the truce by the English. Eventually Charles VII lost patience with diplomatic overtures that seemed to be leading nowhere, and laid siege to Le Mans in late February or early March 1448. There were some skirmishes between the besieging troops and the garrison, but it quickly became apparent that the town would not be able to hold out and relief was unlikely to be forthcoming. Rather than risk everything if the town were taken by storm the garrison surrendered on 15 March 1448. They were allowed safe conduct to depart with all their goods, and the commanders were given money by the French in compensation for the surrender of the town.[3] In view of the promise of Henry VI to cede Maine to Charles VII, the recourse to force to achieve the

---

2   Basin, *Histoire de Charles VII et Louis XI*, pp.219–21.
3   Monstrelet, *Chroniques*, vol.10, pp.112.

handover was not treated as a breakdown of the truce. Indeed, on the day that Le Mans was transferred to him, Charles granted a two-year extension to the truce, to run until 1 April 1450.

The terms of the truce prohibited the construction of new fortifications, in both fortresses and towns, and also the repair of existing defences. However, the Duke of Suffolk, amongst others, as early as 1445 had urged the resupplying with munitions and victuals, which was permitted, as a hedge against a potential outbreak of conflict. However, Henry VI was a profligate spender with a habit of giving generous gifts to courtiers and nobles; he had also spent huge sums on his wedding to Margaret and maintained a large household. He simply did not have the resources to finance the measures needed without the support of Parliament. Unfortunately for English fortunes, the political will was absent, and the English Parliament refused to grant subsidies for use in France. To add to the problem, in Normandy the Estates-General took the opportunity of the peace to reduce taxes which were required for defence. With reduced resources available, not only were towns and castles not restocked but also garrisons were reduced in size. Furthermore, even with reduced garrisons the funding was often not there to pay the men. This created yet another problem: the truce prohibited garrisons living off the land surrounding castles and towns – known as *appâtis*. As one contemporary French observer observed, the first two years of the peace were relatively peaceful but with wages either delayed or not forthcoming at all, either soldiers turned to illegal *appâtis* or captains expropriated taxes to pay their men. This turned many hitherto loyal Normans against the English administration and led to French reprisals. The joint commissioners appointed to resolve disputes over breaches of the truce were powerless to stop the practice and rarely awarded compensation, thus exacerbating ill feeling.[4]

The English resorting to taking what they needed from the countryside and the local population, and the consequent inevitable complaints by the French about breaches of the truce suited Charles VII well. While the English neglected their defences, the King was able to build a case to argue that the English were not adhering to the truce while at the same time he was restructuring his army and preparing for war.

It did nothing to help the English cause that the post of lieutenant-general had been vacant since the Duke of York's departure in September 1445. Edmund Beaufort, promoted to Duke of Somerset just before he took post, arrived in France in May 1448, two months after the surrender of Le Mans – 15 months after his appointment! By the time Somerset arrived the result of the neglect of the defence of English held territory was stark: the number of men deployed in garrisons had fallen from 3,500 before the truce to a mere 2,100.[5] With no English field army deployed in Normandy the

---

4   Basin, *Histoire de Charles VII et Louis XI*, pp.217–9.
5   Juliet Barker, *Conquest, The English Kingdom of France 1417–50* (London: Little, Brown, 2009), p.360.

AN UNEASY PEACE, THE TRUCE OF TOURS 1444-49

balance of forces was moving inexorably in favour of France as the reforms of Charles VII took effect and the truce became increasingly fragile.

From early 1449, French breaches of the truce were becoming more and more frequent and serious, and the lieutenant-general for Normandy had frequent cause to complain of French violations. However, it was the English seizure of the town and castle of Fougères that proved the turning point and the catalyst for the final collapse of the truce. The attack in March 1449 by 600 men was masterminded by François de Surienne, an Aragonese in the service of England and, since 1447, a member of the Order of the Garter. English officials portrayed the attack as being carried out by an independent mercenary captain and denied all knowledge of the operation. In truth, the plans had been laid with the connivance of the English both in London and in Normandy. The motives for the attack were probably mixed. It may have been that an objective was to free the Duke of Brittany's brother Gilles who had been imprisoned for being considered too close to the English cause, particularly since he had been raised alongside Henry VI and received a pension from England. It is also possible that it was chosen as a target because it had formerly belonged to the Duke of Alençon before he was compelled to mortgage it to the Duke of Brittany to pay his ransom after being captured at the Battle of Verneuil in 1424. He had never forgiven Charles VII for failing to support his plans to recover Fougères and he had been out of favour with the French King since 1440. He had conspired with the English on several occasions, and this may have been seen as a way of both rewarding him and tying him to the English cause.

Fougères was in Brittany close to the border of Normandy. In addition to capturing the town and castle Surienne's men, both English and Normans, had ravaged the surrounding countryside.[6] Brittany was not a party to the Truce of Tours, but the attack was nevertheless treated as any other breach of the truce. An outraged Duke of Brittany demanded the return of the town and castle and reparations. When his demands were refused, he turned to Charles VII who was only too happy to take up the cause. Whatever the motives for the seizure of Fougères the issue was now being turned against the English. While Charles protested to the Duke of Somerset, he also authorised retaliatory attacks on English territory.

The Tour St-Vigor on the ramparts of Pont-de-l'Arche. (Peter Hoskins)

---

6   Chartier, *Chronique de Charles VII, Roi de* France, vol.2, pp.60–61.

THE BATTLE OF CASTILLON 1453

In May 1449, while English and French ambassadors were at Louviers trying to resolve the situation concerning Fougères, the French took the strategically important town of Pont-de-l'Arche, by subterfuge. This seizure was rapidly followed by the capture of nearby Conches and Gerberoy. Somerset sent Shrewsbury to Pont-Audemer to the west of Pont-de-l'Arche, but he would not risk a confrontation in case this destroyed hopes of saving the truce. When the English protested, Charles played the card that they had used for Fougères – denying all knowledge and claiming that the captain concerned was acting without orders and simply expressing his frustration at English breaches of the truce. Indeed, when Somerset sent heralds to Pont-de-l'Arche to ask the French commanders if they had acted for the King of France or on his orders, they replied that they were acting for the Duke of Brittany and were merely seeking compensation for the loss of Fougères.[7] However, Charles VII had actually given a secret undertaking to the Duke of Brittany that if the English had not returned Fougères to him by the end of July he would give him his full support and renew the war.[8] While the main focus was on Normandy, with the connivance of the Duke of Brittany, a Gascon took the English castles of Saint-Thomas-de-Conac and Saint-Maigrin in Aquitaine, by escalade.[9] The Duke of Somerset sent an envoy to Charles VII at Chinon to protest and demand the return of the towns. The reply was, as to be expected, that this was a matter between Brittany and England, but that Charles was sure that if Fougères were returned to the Duke he would be happy to return Saint-Thomas-de-Conac and Saint-Maigrin to English jurisdiction.[10]

Meanwhile, messengers had been sent to England to impress upon Parliament the parlous situation in Normandy and to press for money. In the event, in July Parliament eventually granted funds but, apparently indifferent to the developing French threat, not for use in Normandy.

During May and June negotiations over breaches of the truce, and, in particular, Fougères, continued. The negotiations were soured by the seizure by the English in late April of a fleet of ships carrying Breton salt, but flying under the flags of the Dutch, the Flemish and the Hanseatic League (all friendly towards England). This act of aggression incensed the Duke of Brittany who, already angered by the lack of progress over Fougères, now committed himself to the support of Charles VII. In May the Duke and Charles made a defensive and offensive alliance and the Bretons started to prepare for war. This added another dispute to the agenda since Henry VI and Charles VII both claimed sovereignty over Brittany. Somerset now

---

7   Basin, *Histoire de Charles VII et Louis XI*, pp.233–4.
8   Chartier, *Chronique de Charles VII, Roi de* France, vol.2, pp.69–74.
9   Chartier records the two strongholds as being Conat or Cognat and Saint-Malgrin or Saint-Maulgrin. Conat/Cognat is often assumed to have been Cognac. This is impossible. Cognac had fallen to Du Guesclin in 1375 following a siege and had remained in French hands ever since. It is probable that these places were Saint-Thomas-de-Conac and Saint-Maigrin.
10 Chartier, *Chronique de Charles VII, Roi de* France, vol.2, pp.74–5.

used this to justify the attack on Fougères as an issue between England and Brittany and nothing to do with France; hence it could not be considered a violation of the truce. Unsurprisingly Charles took a different view and argued that Somerset was simply using this argument to prevent a settlement being found. Somerset seemed to see the Fougères dispute as being parallel with that over Pont-de-l'Arche and Gerberoy and that the negotiations were simply a prolongation of those that had been going on over breaches of the truce for some years. He was oblivious of the fact that the French were using the talks to cover their mobilisation.

Charles VII met with his council on 17 July at the castle of Roches-Tranchelion, 25 miles south-west of Tours in the Loire Valley. The decision was taken to return to war.[11] Armies were already gathering for a three-pronged assault on English held territory: from Brittany into Lower Normandy, through the centre, and from Picardy into Upper Normandy. On 20 July, the town of Verneuil-d'Avre-et-d'Iton was betrayed to a French force. The English garrison retreated into the Grey Tower, which was strong and eminently defensible, but short of provisions. Word had been sent to Rouen of the parlous situation and Shrewsbury set off with a relief force. However, in the meantime the Bastard of Orléans had arrived at Verneuil with substantial reinforcements. Shrewsbury was now faced with a much stronger force than he had anticipated, and after initially drawing up his force in a defensive position within a circle of wagons, he withdrew to Rouen and left the garrison to their fate – including, with perhaps some poetic justice, François de Surienne who had taken Fougères only four months before.[12]

The seizure of Verneuil as far as the English were concerned, as yet unaware of the French decision taken three days before to renounce the truce, was yet another violation of the truce to add to the catalogue of breaches. However, all this was now irrelevant. On 31 July 1449, English envoys were summoned to meet with Charles VII. The King berated them with a list of perceived English transgressions since the arrival of Somerset as lieutenant-general and declared that he felt freed from his obligations under the truce – the renewal of war was now official. The English had made the fundamental error of assuming that the French shared their preference for a peaceful settlement over war. While the English had fatally neglected their military capability the French had used the five years of truce to prepare their armies. The English and their remaining allies were quickly to pay the price for their negligence and complacency.

---

11 Basin, *Histoire de Charles VII et Louis XI*, pp.236, n.3.
12 Gilles le Bouvier, ed. Alain Chartier, *L'Histoire Mémorable des Grands Troubles de ce Royaume sous le Roi Charles VII*, (Nevers: Pierre Roussin, 1594), pp.138–9; Barker, *Conquest, The English Kingdom of France*, p.381.

5

The Reconquest of Normandy 1449–50

Once the Treaty of Tours had finally been renounced by Charles VII on 31 July 1449 events moved quickly. The French were organised in three armies: the Duke of Brittany moved into Normandy from the west, the Counts of Eu and Saint-Pol entered the duchy from the east, crossing the Seine at Pont-de-l'Arche and the King came north from the Loire.

On 8 August, Eu and Saint-Pol reached the castle of Nogent-Pré. Surrounded by a much greater force and with little or no hope of relief, after a brief resistance the small Anglo-Norman garrison surrendered the next day and were allowed to leave with all their possessions except for their arms and equipment. The castle was set alight before the departure of the French army.[1] In the following days this force of around 4,000 men was reinforced by 2,000 men under the command of Jean de Dunois (the Bastard of Orléans), the Lord of Gaucourt and Poton de Xaintrailles coming from Évreux. The combined force surrounded the town of Pont-Audemer, about nine miles south of the river Seine and 12 miles south-east of Honfleur.

The town lay to the south of the small river Risle. The defences of the town were in a poor state, in part consisting of only of a wooden palisade, although the south of the town was protected by a deep water-filled moat. The Counts of Eu and Saint-Pol took position on the north bank of the river, while Dunois arrayed his men to the south of the town. The town garrison, recently reinforced by Fulk Eyton and Osbern Mundeford, the Treasurer of Normandy, was probably between 400 and 500 strong. The French had no siege equipment but decided to attempt to take the town by assault, apparently unaware of the strength of the garrison. It appears that the attack started almost by accident. An archer shot a burning arrow towards the town that ignited a thatched roof and the fire spread rapidly.

---

1 Chartier, *Chronique de Charles VII, Roi de* France, vol.2, pp.84–5. The location of Nogent-Pré is uncertain, but it was probably close to Pont-de-l'Arche.

THE RECONQUEST OF NORMANDY 1449-50

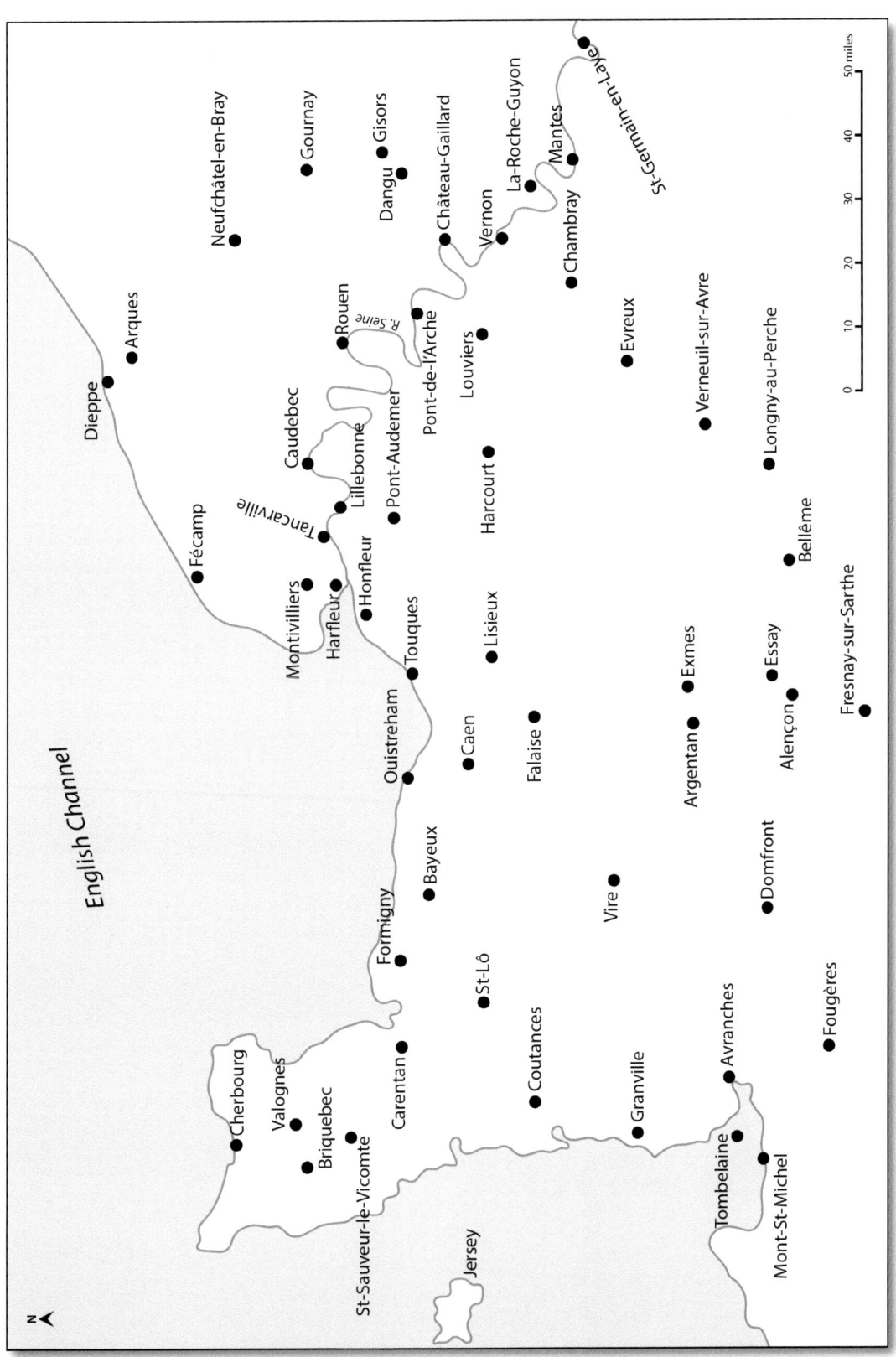

The French re-conquest of Normandy, 1449-50

THE BATTLE OF CASTILLON 1453

The Cathedral of St-Pierre in Lisieux, Bishop Basin was instrumental in negotiating the town's surrender to the French and went on to serve King Charles VII. (Peter Hoskins)

The opportunity was seized to launch the assault with Dunois' men forcing an entry despite having to wade through water up to their armpits. The fighting was fierce, with a number of French squires earning their knighthoods. With the garrison driven back and surrounded it became clear that further resistance would only lead to more loss of life. The garrison surrendered on 12 August with Eyton and Mundeford becoming prisoners.[2]

From Pont-Audemer the French continued 20 miles to the south-west to Lisieux. According to the chronicler Thomas Basin, who was bishop of the town at the time, the town was poorly defended. The English garrison was only around 100 strong and the town had neither ditches nor walls for protection. Basin recounts that he recognised the weaknesses of the town and called together the clergy and town council to offer to negotiate a surrender. He records that the French host was more than 10,000 strong, and, although this may have been an exaggeration, it is undeniable that the situation of the English garrison was hopeless. Basin, a Norman by birth, had held a chair of canonical law at the University of Caen in Normandy since 1441 before becoming Bishop of Lisieux in 1447. He was clearly correct in his analysis of the situation, but having been in a prominent position in Norman life for the past few years probably saw the way things were going and his action clearly served his self-interest. He quickly became close to the French court, becoming a councillor to Charles VII, and Basin delivered an address when the victorious King entered Rouen a little over two months later. Basin gives a detailed account of the surrender of Lisieux. The terms, the precedent for which had been set at Pont-Audemer, are worth recalling here in some detail since they became the form for subsequent surrenders. They also demonstrate that Charles had astutely decided on a policy of winning hearts and minds among the Norman population, rather than extracting revenge on those who had fought for the English and were considered 'renegade French'.

---

2   Chartier, *Chronique de Charles VII, Roi de* France, vol.2, pp.85–7. Barker, *Conquest, The English Kingdom of France*, p.382. Basin, *Histoire de Charles VII et Louis XI*, pp.236–8.

The English civilian residents were offered two choices: they could remain and, having sworn an oath of loyalty to the French King, retain their property and continue to benefit from all the rights to which they had been accustomed, or they could leave safely with all their portable goods or sell them if they preferred. Those who chose to leave could, before their departure, enforce any debts owing to them, but if they owed money, they were also required to settle their debts within four days of the surrender. The garrison was allowed to depart freely under a safe conduct. Normans who had fought for the English were pardoned and accepted back into the French fold. The surrender of Lisieux brought with it the transfer of seven castles to French authority.[3]

On 23 August 1449, the garrison of Grey Tower in Verneuil surrendered, having held out for five weeks, despite Shrewsbury having failed to resupply the garrison. Within the tower the French found only 30 men, the majority of whom were French. The rest, including Jean de Surienne, had managed to escape taking anything of value, including money, with them. This was much to the annoyance of Charles VII, who had given specific orders to the commander of the besieging force to be on his guard against escapes by the garrison. However, once again the King stuck to his policy of pardoning renegades and allowing the garrison to depart freely.[4]

According to Basin the French commanders took counsel after the fall of Lisieux and asked his advice on the best course of action. It was decided that the King should next take Mantes-la-Jolie, on the Seine 30 miles north-west of Paris. This made a good deal of sense. Mantes would serve as a good secure base to which to bring supplies down river from Paris. From here the French could proceed downstream with the intention of taking Rouen, the centre of English administration in Normandy. As the French progressed, other towns and castles could be expected to fall to the French.

The surviving perimeter tower of St-Martin on the town walls of Mantes-la-Jolie. (Peter Hoskins)

---

3   Chartier, *Chronique de Charles VII, Roi de* France, vol.2, pp.93–4. Barker, *Conquest, The English Kingdom of France*, p.383. Basin, *Histoire de Charles VII et Louis XI*, pp.238–41.
4   Chartier, *Chronique de Charles VII, Roi de* France, vol.2, pp.92–3. Barker, *Conquest, The English Kingdom of France*, p.383–4.

Charles VII sent a herald to Mantes to call for its surrender. In the absence of the English Captain of the town, Sir Thomas Hoo, his lieutenant Thomas de Saint-Barbe, with a reported garrison of 260 men, was inclined to defend the town. The mayor and population had other ideas and seized one of the gates, which they threatened to open and allow the French to enter. The garrison surrendered on 26 August. Similar terms as had been accorded to the English garrison and inhabitants of Lisieux were agreed.[5]

On 3 September, the castle at La-Roche-Guyon also surrendered, allegedly in return for a promise that the English captain could hold on to the lands of his French wife. La-Roche-Guyon was evacuated on 12 September.[6] The castle is not large, but it is in a strategically important position only about 250 yards from the river, eight miles north-west of Mantes. It stands on high ground and had proved difficult to take in the past. In 1418, it had resisted the English for four months. Its surrender now removed a potential threat to the passage of French shipping downstream from Mantes.

Charles VII arrived at Verneuil on 27 August, the day after the fall of Mantes-la-Jolie, and the day after, Vernon surrendered to Dunois. Once again, the attitude of the population had been decisive in the decision to surrender. When the French initially called for the surrender of the keys of the town and the castle of Les Tourelles in Vernonnet the captain had contemptuously given the French herald a bunch of rusty keys. With a garrison reported to be 600 strong he believed that he was in a strong position and was determined to hold the town, which stands on the left bank of the Seine with the castle of Les Tourelles on the right bank, protecting the bridge over the river. However, when *franc-archers* took an island in the river and subsequently the bridge the inhabitants of the town announced that they would surrender the town whether the English agreed or not. In the face of this unfavourable situation the English captain agreed to surrender, but on condition that the garrison were given letters explaining that they had given up the town and castle against their will. They also asked, as was common, for a short delay to allow for the arrival of a relief force from Rouen. This not being forthcoming, they duly surrendered and were allowed to march out and return to English held territory.[7]

The problem of lack of relief for besieged towns and fortresses was symptomatic of the weakness of the English position. The men that they had were dispersed in penny packets as garrisons. There were insufficient men to form a field army; a reinforcement force of 1,300 men from England had been promised for June 1449 but had not materialised, with only some

---

5 Chartier, *Chronique de Charles VII, Roi de* France, vol.2, pp.94–101. Basin, *Histoire de Charles VII et Louis XI*, pp.236–8.
6 David Nicolle, *The Fall of English France 1449–53* (Oxford: Osprey, 2012), p.23. Fresne de Beaucourt, G. du, *Histoire de Charles VII*, vol.5, *Le Roi Victorieux 1449–53* (Paris: Alphonse Picard, 1890), p.9, n.1.
7 Chartier, *Chronique de Charles VII, Roi de* France, vol.2, pp.103–9.

THE RECONQUEST OF NORMANDY 1449–50

The Castle of Les Tourelles in Vernonnet on the right bank of the Seine across the river from Vernon. (Peter Hoskins)

450 men mustering for service at the end of July.⁸ In the circumstances the redoubtable and normally aggressive John Talbot, Earl of Shrewsbury, could not risk the defence of Rouen by drawing on the garrison for relief forces.

Around the same time a minor castle at Longny-au-Perche passed into French hands. This was of little military significance but indicative of the collapse of Norman allegiance to the English administration. The captain of the castle, François de Surienne, was absent but his wife was present. Surienne had entrusted the castle's defence to his son-in-law, the Norman Richard aux-Épaules, with a garrison of 200 men. Aux-Épaules accepted the substantial sum of 12,000 *écus* to allow the French to enter the keep, and he stood by as the brief resistance was overcome. The garrison was probably largely made up of Surienne's mercenaries, since aux-Épaules later received money to distribute among 12 French-speaking members of the garrison who had supported him. The remainder were made prisoner. Surienne's wife, who understandably was less than happy with her son-in-law's behaviour, was sent on her way with her belongings. Aux-Épaules swore alliance to Charles VII and accepted the captaincy of the castle. The circumstances suggest that aux-Épaule's conduct was driven mainly by self-interest, and it is unlikely that he would have acted thus if the English had still been in a position of strength in the duchy.⁹ The captain of La-Roche-Guyon surrendered his castle for personal reasons, and a similar example was to follow in October with the surrender of Gisors. The captain, Richard

---

8   Barker, *Conquest, The English Kingdom of France*, p.389.
9   Chartier, *Chronique de Charles VII, Roi de* France, vol.2, pp.101–3. Barker, *Conquest, The English Kingdom of France*, pp.386–7. Basin, *Histoire de Charles VII et Louis XI*, pp.238–41.

Merbury, who had been a member of the Duke of Bedford's household, surrendered the castle in return for the release without ransom of his two sons who had been taken prisoner previously. He did not remain as captain of Gisors but was appointed by Charles VII as captain of Saint-Germain-en-Laye. He was also allowed to retain the lands of his French wife.[10]

The fall of English held fortresses and towns continued at an astonishing pace. At the end of August Louviers and Évreux opened their gates to the French. Gournay and the castle at Dangu also surrendered. During September numerous other towns and castles went over to the French, either voluntarily or following short sieges. The towns of Touques, Essay, Exmes (late September), Alençon, Chambray (20 September) and Argentan (4 October) fell without a fight. At Dieppe the French garrison sallied out and took Fécamp by surprise, capturing as they did so 97 soldiers on a ship entering the port unaware that the town had fallen to the French.[11] Meanwhile the Duke of Brittany had entered the fray with 6,000 men and taken Coutances, Granville, Carentan, Saint-Lô and Valognes.[12] In the last fortnight of September, 11 castles in the Carentan surrendered to the Duke of Brittany's army.[13]

Despite all this gloom for the English cause there were examples of stubborn resistance, notably the castle of Harcourt, 25 miles south-west of Rouen. The garrison, commanded by Richard Frogenhalle, was about 150 strong. There was skirmishing with casualties on both sides, but as the siege progressed it became apparent to Frogenhalle that with the artillery being deployed there was little point in continuing to resist. A composition was negotiated with the besiegers. If no help were forthcoming to relieve the garrison, they would surrender the castle. After 15 days of resistance, they left under safe conduct leaving the French to take possession of the castle on 14 Sep 1449.[14] The captain of Neufchâtel-en-Bray, 25 miles north-east of Rouen, also put up some resistance. The town fell quickly after the arrival of the French but the 150 or so men in the garrison held out in the castle for a fortnight before surrendering and marching out under a safe conduct.[15]

The situation for Rouen was looking increasingly precarious. The French now held towns and fortresses surrounding the city, from Dieppe to the north, Neufchâtel to the north-east, Gournay to the east, Gisors to the south-east, Louviers and Vernon to the south, Pont-Audemer to the west and Fécamp to the north-west. Delivering supplies to the city would be increasingly problematic. In early October the combined French armies of Dunois, the Counts of Eu and de Saint-Pol, René d'Anjou and Raoul de

---

10   Barker, *Conquest, The English Kingdom of France*, p.387.
11   Chartier, *Chronique de Charles VII, Roi de* France, vol.2, pp.112–15. Barker, *Conquest, The English Kingdom of France*, p.388–9.
12   Philippe Bully, *Charles VII, le "Rois des Merveilles"*, (Paris: Tallendier, 1994), p.265.
13   Beaucourt, *Histoire de Charles VII*, vol.5, p.9.
14   Chartier, *Chronique de Charles VII, Roi de* France, vol.2, pp.115–6. Fresne de Beaucourt, *Histoire de Charles VII*, vol.5, p.8.
15   Chartier, *Chronique de Charles VII, Roi de* France, vol.2, pp.119–20.

THE RECONQUEST OF NORMANDY 1449-50

Gaucourt began to converge on Rouen. While Charles VII was at Louviers, some inhabitants of Rouen came to see the King, and they reported that a great part of the population was plotting against the English. If the French came to the walls of the town, inhabitants on duty on the walls would ensure their safe entry. The King is reported to have been distrustful, suspecting a trap. However, having taken counsel with his commanders he decided to attempt to take Rouen by storm, despite the significant garrison and strong defences. On 16 October Dunois led a scaling party over a section of wall between two towers held by townspeople sympathetic to the French cause. Shrewsbury led a determined, and effective, counterattack with 300 men that resulted in 50 or 60 French, including some of the inhabitants who had helped them enter the town, being either captured or killed as the attack was repulsed.

However, the townspeople were not inclined to suffer a long siege. Many had memories of the long and terrible siege of 1418–19 when the town had fallen to the English. They were also conscious that neither food supplies nor firewood had entered Rouen for six weeks, and with the distant encirclement of the town and the large besieging force, the position was unlikely to improve. They had nothing to look forward but another dreadful siege. The day after the failed French assault, the inhabitants demanded that Edmund Beaufort, Duke of Somerset, allow the archbishop to negotiate a surrender on their behalf. Somerset had little choice but to agree. However, when the terms of surrender were brought to him, he judged them to be unacceptable, although they were more generous than the terms that he finally accepted. The population was outraged and rebelled, driving the English back towards the fortified gate guarding the bridge, the castle, and the palace, harassing them as they withdrew. The townsmen then opened the city gates to Dunois. The garrison guarding the bridge was compelled to surrender on 20 October.

With the French in control of the town Somerset, Shrewsbury, and Thomas Hoo were now confined to the palace and the castle. Within the castle and the palace was a substantial garrison of 1,200 men, many of whom had come from other towns and castles that had surrendered. However, food was in short supply and in view of the strength of the besieging force, which was well equipped with artillery, there was little choice for the English

The keep of Rouen castle, now known as the Tour de Jeanne d'Arc. (Peter Hoskins)

other than to negotiate their way out of the predicament. The problem for Somerset was that the French held all the cards and Charles VII was not going to be satisfied with letting him and his men march away.

Following attacks on 22 October, Somerset decided to open negotiations, and met with Charles VII the following day. The terms offered were more severe than those previously proposed, but Somerset now had little room for manoeuvre. On 29 October 1449, after having met with Charles VII a second time to settle the terms, Somerset put his seal to the surrender of Rouen. In sealing the surrender, Somerset also agreed to the surrender of six other places still in English hands: Caudebec, Tancarville, Lillebonne, Harfleur, Montivilliers, and Arques, and he agreed to pay a ransom of 50,000 *écus* within a year. As guarantors of the terms eight prominent men were handed over to the French as hostages, including Shrewsbury and Richard Gower, the son of Thomas Gower, captain of Cherbourg. In return Somerset and his family, and anyone else who wished to do so, could leave under a safe conduct and return to England. They were free to take their possessions, but all heavy artillery was to be left behind, and all debts due to the inhabitants were to be settled before departure. The chronicler Thomas Basin recorded that these debts amounted to 100,000 *livres* but in the end went unpaid, senior French nobles being content to accept generous presents from their English counterparts at the expense of the town's tradesmen. On 4 November 1449, Somerset left the town.

The keep and southern end of Arques castle. (Peter Hoskins)

The reaction in England was one of outrage. Not only had the principal English held town in Normandy surrendered meekly without a fight after little more than two weeks of siege, but other towns and fortresses had been surrendered when they were not directly threatened. Somerset embarked at Harfleur and headed for Caen, having perhaps reflected on his surrender and fearing an accusation, and a trial, for treason if he returned to England.[16]

The day after Somerset left Rouen another town surrendered. This time it was the turn of François de Surienne to give the

---

16   Chartier, *Chronique de Charles VII, Roi de* France, vol.2, pp.137–60. Barker, *Conquest, The English Kingdom of France*, pp.390–1. Basin, *Histoire de Charles VII et Louis XI*, pp.249–54. Fresne de Beaucourt, *Histoire de Charles VII*, vol.5, pp.16–18.

THE RECONQUEST OF NORMANDY 1449-50

keys of Fougères to the Duke of Brittany. He claimed that he had held out for five weeks under heavy bombardment. He also complained that many of his men had deserted and that he had been promised reinforcements by the English Government that had not materialised. Towards the end of September 400 men had arrived in Normandy from England but had been persuaded to remain in Caen to reinforce its garrison. De Surienne accepted 10,000 *écus* for the surrender of the town. Much embittered he resigned his membership of the Order of the Garter, entered the service of the Duke of Burgundy and was eventually naturalised to become a subject of the King of France.[17]

Events continued to move quickly with the fortress of Bellême surrendering on 20 November and with the supposedly impregnable Château-Gaillard following three days later after a siege of five weeks.

The implications of the fall of Rouen and the rapidly deteriorating situation in Normandy were finally realised in England. In late November, arms were sent to Caen and Cherbourg, including 1,000 bows, 2,880 bowstrings, 2,000 sheaves of arrows and 1,800lbs of gunpowder. Ten days later, on 4 December 1449, Sir Thomas Kyriell was contracted to take 425 men-at-arms and 2,080 archers to Normandy. That was easier said than done and the Treasurer was forced to pawn the crown jewels to raise money, although the sum raised was not sufficient and loans were required from

The Rouen Gate on the perimeter wall of Harfleur. (Peter Hoskins)

---

17 Chartier, *Chronique de Charles VII, Roi de* France, vol.2, pp.172–3. Barker, *Conquest, The English Kingdom of France*, pp.391–3.

Cardinal Beaufort and the Duke of Suffolk. However, the money was slow forthcoming and, without pay, the troops rioted as they waited to board ship in Portsmouth. In the end, Sir Thomas Kyriell and his men did not arrive in Cherbourg until 15 March 1450. As events were to prove the arms and reinforcements were too little too late.[18]

While the English were struggling to raise reinforcements at home, the situation in Normandy continued to move in favour of the French. On 8 December, Dunois arrived outside Harfleur with around 10,000 men, including 4,000 *franc-archers* and 16 heavy bombards. The garrison held out for a little over a fortnight before, on Christmas Eve, recognising their hopeless situation, and began negotiations. The captain of the town agreed to surrender on 1 January 1450. The French took eight hostages as a guarantee of good faith, unsurprising since Harfleur should have been surrendered under the conditions of the surrender of Rouen. The hostages were released on 1 January when the keys were handed over to the French; the garrison was allowed to leave with their possessions. There were so many English in the town, including 1,600 men in the garrison and a further 400 who had come from other garrisons, that two days were allowed for evacuation by sea.

The chroniclers recorded that the winter of 1449–50 was particularly harsh. It is perhaps indicative of Charles VII's determination to finish the campaign as quickly as possible, and before the English had the chance to gather their will and their strength, that he nevertheless relentlessly continued his campaign.[19] From Harfleur Dunois turned his attention to Honfleur, which was defended by a garrison of 400 men. The siege was set on 17 January 1450 and the town and castle resisted until, in due course, following a two-day bombardment which destroyed much of the defences of the town, a composition was made with the French that, if relief was not forthcoming by 18 February, the town and castle would surrender. The French were sufficiently concerned about the prospect of Somerset bringing a relief force from Caen that they entrenched their positions. However, Somerset did not stir, and the English garrison left the town on the agreed date.[20]

The collapse of English Normandy continued into the spring. In March, the French arrived before the castle of Fresnay-le-Vicomte (now Fresnay-sur-Sarthe) with a large force, well equipped with artillery. The 400 or 500 strong garrison of English and Norman troops decided to sue for surrender, and on 22 March 1450, left under a safe conduct.[21]

---

18 Barker, *Conquest, The English Kingdom of France*, pp.392, Nicolle, *The Fall of English France*, p.41.
19 Chartier, *Chronique de Charles VII, Roi de* France, vol.2, pp.176–81. Barker, *Conquest, The English Kingdom of France*, pp.394.
20 Chartier, *Chronique de Charles VII, Roi de* France, vol.2, pp.188–9, Basin, *Histoire de Charles VII et Louis XI*, p.255.
21 Chartier, *Chronique de Charles VII, Roi de* France, vol.2, pp.189–90.

Plate A
The Earl of Shrewsbury
(Illustration by Giorgio Albertini © Helion & Company)
See Colour Plate Commentaries for further information.

Plate B
Sir Thomas Everyingham
(Illustration by Giorgio Albertini © Helion & Company)
See Colour Plate Commentaries for further information.

**Plate C
French Crossbowman**
(Illustration by Giorgio Albertini © Helion & Company)
See Colour Plate Commentaries for further information.

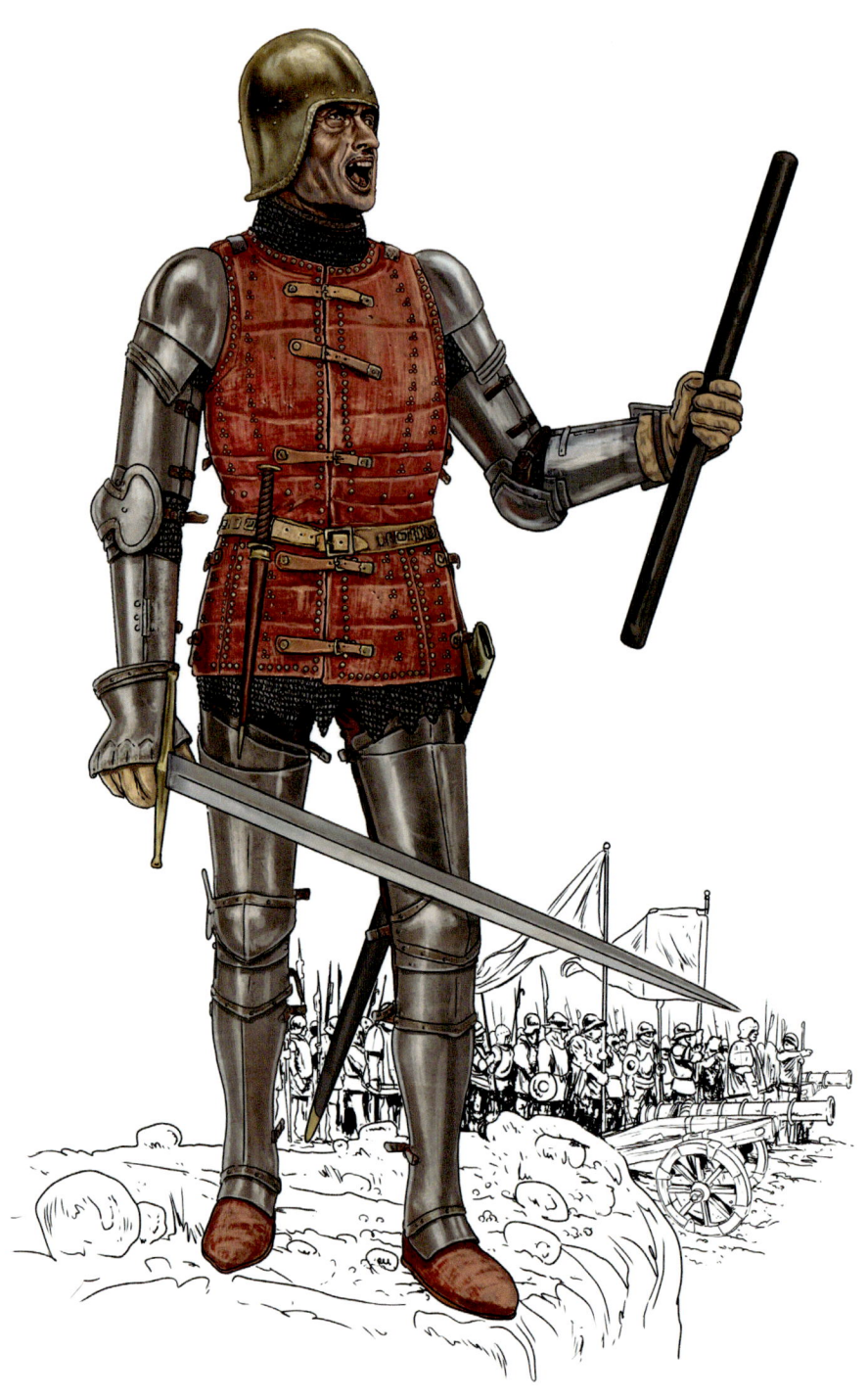

**Plate D
Jean Bureau**
(Illustration by Giorgio Albertini © Helion & Company)
See Colour Plate Commentaries for further information.

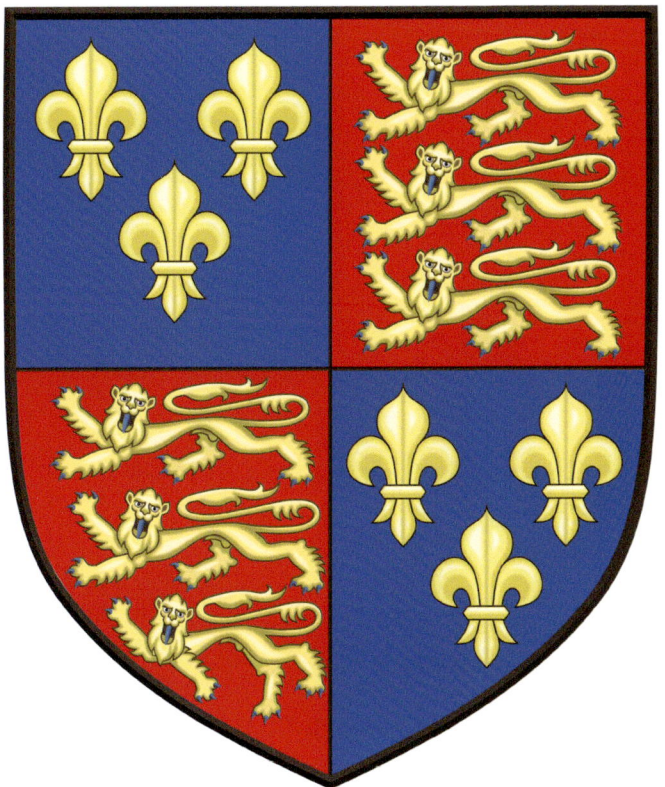

Plate E
1 The Royal Arms of England during the reign of Henry VI
2 The arms of John Talbot, First Earl of Shrewsbury
(Illustrations by Anderson Subtil © Helion & Company)
See Colour Plate Commentaries for further information.

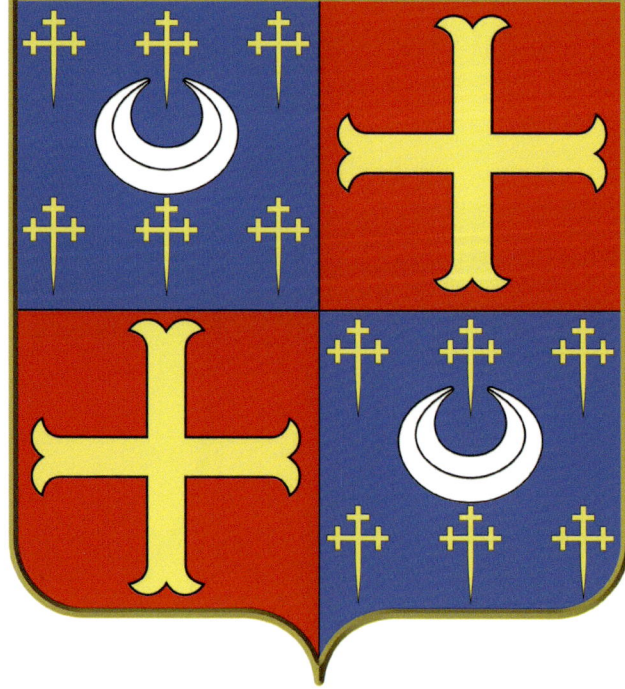

Plate F
1 The Trinity Banner. 2 The arms of Jean V de Bueil.
(Illustrations by Anderson Subtil © Helion & Company)
See Colour Plate Commentaries for further information.

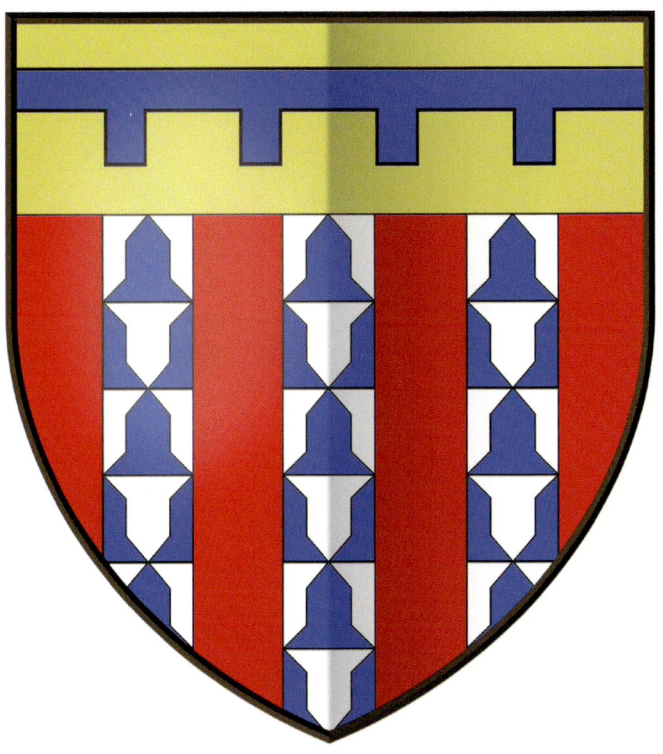

Plate G
1 The arms of Jean IV de Châtillon, Count of Penthièvre.
2 The arms of Jacques V de Chabannes.
(Illustrations by Anderson Subtil © Helion & Company)
See Colour Plate Commentaries for further information.

Plate H
1 The arms of Jean de Foix-Grailly, Viscount of Castillon and Earl of Kendal.
2 The arms of Jean Bureau.
(Illustrations by Anderson Subtil © Helion & Company)
See Colour Plate Commentaries for further information.

THE RECONQUEST OF NORMANDY 1449-50

However, despite the fall of many towns and strongholds to the French, the English still held, with significant garrisons, the great towns of Caen, Bayeux, and Falaise. Parts of the Cotentin peninsular including the port of Cherbourg were also still in English hands. It was at Cherbourg that Thomas Kyriell finally arrived with his army on 15 March 1450. It appears that his orders were to support Bayeux. However, 11 miles south-east of Cherbourg on his line of march stood the town and castle of Valognes, garrisoned by the French. To bypass Valognes and leave it occupied by the French would pose a serious threat to his lines of communication and Kyriell decided that it was necessary to subdue Valognes before moving on towards Bayeux. The Duke of Somerset was of the same opinion and sent Kyriell men from the remaining English garrisons. To Kyriell's army of 2,500 men, which had brought a large artillery train suggesting the objective of retaking towns and fortresses which had fallen to the French, were added 600 men from Caen under the command of Robert Vere, 800 from Bayeux under Matthew Gough, and 400 from Vire under Henry Norbury.

The captain of the garrison at Valognes sent an urgent message to the French commanders for help. Kyriell, however, had moved quickly to lay siege to the town within a few days of arriving in Normandy. Having lodged in Cherbourg Abbey overnight he had set out the day after the landing, a remarkable achievement given the time required to unload stores and horses. He brought with him artillery from Cherbourg.[22] The French were well aware of the landing of the English and the despatch of the men from other English garrisons to join him. However, their forces were dispersed across Brittany and Normandy. They could not muster sufficient strength in time to challenge Kyriell's army, now of between 4,000 and 5,000 men, before the situation became critical at Valognes. The garrison held out for three weeks, but when no help was forthcoming surrendered on 10 April 1450; they were allowed to leave taking their belongings with them. Kyriell had lost valuable time at Valognes, but now set out towards Bayeux and Caen, where according to the chronicler Thomas Basin, Somerset was waiting to form a field army large enough to meet the French in battle.[23]

Kyriell now faced two choices for his onward march: he could either take the main road, which would entail taking the town of Carentan, still in French hands, or cross the marshland and estuary of the river Douve at the Grand-Vey. Taking Carentan would take time once again and additionally would risk his being caught in an unfavourable position by the French as their forces converged on the English line of march. He opted for the second option and set out on 12 April. The crossing of the estuary was a risky undertaking; sands and marshes extended about four miles in front of the river and its two fords, which are about three miles apart. The army

---

22 Monstrelet, *Chroniques*, vol.10, pp.248-9.
23 Barker, *Conquest, The English Kingdom of France*, pp.394-5, Nicolle, *The Fall of English France*, pp.26-8, Chartier, *Chronique de Charles VII, Roi de* France, vol.2, pp.191-2, Basin, *Histoire de Charles VII et Louis XI*, pp.255-7.

would be vulnerable as it was strung out in columns to cross the Douve. However, with a new moon on 15 April and the associated spring tide, the conditions for the crossing were much more favourable than they would have been at other dates in the lunar cycle, giving six or seven hours to make a safe crossing. The Count of Clermont, at Carentan with 500 or 600 lances (between 3,000 and 3,600 men-at-arms) and an unspecified number of archers, sent a small force to assist local people who were trying to impede the English crossing. The defenders were brushed aside, and the crossing was completed successfully. On the night of 14 April 1450 Kyriell's army set up camp near Formigny, ten miles beyond the fords and ten miles from Bayeux. Why he and Gough decided to pitch camp here for the night rather than pressing on as far as possible towards Bayeux that day is unknown.. Perhaps he hoped to lure the French onto a strong defensive position. Since Gough left for Bayeux, perhaps he was seeking reinforcements with such an objective in mind.

Clermont caught up with the English near Formigny. He had earlier sent the parish priest from Carentan to the Constable, Arthur de Richemont, who was at Saint-Lô, about 16 miles south-west of Formigny, urging him to move to the village of Trévières some two miles south of Formigny and thus take the English in the flank. De Richemont probably had 1,200 to 1,500 men-at-arms and 800 archers. Kyriell had warning of the progress of the French under Clermont and had sufficient time to take up a strong defensive position with his back to a small river. He also had trenches dug and stakes planted.

Clermont arrived at around midday and his men halted outside of arrow range for three hours; he then sent forward two small cannon, protected by archers and men-at-arms, to fire into the English archers. The archers launched an apparently unauthorised attack, drove off the gunners and protecting force and captured the guns. The French responded with a small number of men-at-arms, but these in turn were driven off by men sent by Kyriell. According to a contemporary French report if the English had launched a full-scale attack now the French would have been in considerable difficulty. However, Gough, who was now back with the English army, and Kyriell elected not to attack but rather to hold their defensive position. The battle had been in progress for some hours when de Richemont arrived at Trévières. The English now had a substantial force on their flank. In the meantime, some of Clermont's men had taken advantage of the confusion to retake the guns lost earlier in the battle. Kyriell and Gough attempted to wheel their left wing to the left to face the new threat, a difficult manoeuvre with the French in contact. De Richemont and Clermont seized the opportunity. The subsequent fighting was confused, but the result was a dramatic defeat for the English. Panic seized the army and little quarter was given in the ensuing combat, with local inhabitants joining in the slaughter. One report talks of 500 archers throwing down their weapons and asking for mercy but being massacred. Gough was able to extricate himself from the chaos and fled to Bayeux with some mounted men. Robert Vere was also able to escape and made his way to Caen. Kyriell and Norbury were

THE RECONQUEST OF NORMANDY 1449-50

among the between 1,200 and 1,400 prisoners.

Heralds, who carried out the traditional task of counting and identifying the dead, recorded the deaths of 3,774 men in the English army who were buried in 14 grave pits. French losses were recorded as eight men killed. This is an improbably low figure, but it was by no means unusual for there to be very disproportionate losses between the victors and the defeated in medieval battles. Once discipline collapsed and panic set in, followed by a rout, a defeated army was extremely vulnerable and risked being cut down in large numbers. Much the same had happened to the French after the victory of the Black Prince at Poitiers in 1356, and there was also a huge disparity between casualties for the two armies at Agincourt in 1415. There is uncertainty over the precise strengths of the English and French armies at Formigny; if the French had a numerical advantage, it was small. Whatever the relative strengths of the armies, this was a disaster for the English on the scale that Agincourt had been for the French; it ended all realistic hope of England holding on to Normandy.[24]

Ramparts at Saint-Lô. (Peter Hoskins)

The defeat at Formigny was a huge shock in England. Sir John Fastolf tried to raise an army of 3,000 men, and in July a large number of arrows was sent to Normandy. It was all too late; events were moving too quickly. After the battle the French moved to Saint-Lô for two or three days to rest, to care for the wounded, and to bury the dead. However, there was to be no respite for what remained of English Normandy. Clermont and Richemont asked whether they should next attack Vire or Bayeux. Charles VII chose Vire, possibly because its captain, Henry Norbury, had been taken prisoner at the Battle of Formigny. The French marched on Vire, 20 miles south of Saint-Lô. Vire had a garrison of 300 to 400 men, but resistance was short-

---

24   Barker, *Conquest, The English Kingdom of France*, pp.395–6. Nicolle, *The Fall of English France*, pp.29–35. Chartier, *Chronique de Charles VII, Roi de France*, vol.2, pp.192–200. Basin, *Histoire de Charles VII et Louis XI*, pp.258–60.

lived, and after six days a composition was made for the surrender of the town. Norbury was released, with the French contributing 4,000 *francs*, towards his ransom and the garrison marched out heading to Caen, with their possessions, around 27 April 1450. They left behind all their artillery.[25]

The French now divided their forces. Clermont headed for Bayeux, 30 miles to the north, to join Dunois, and Richemont set off 25 miles south-west to besiege Avranches. At the end of April or early May, the siege of Bayeux was opened. Both Bureau brothers were present, and they supervised a prolonged and effective bombardment that steadily reduced the walls to rubble. The defence of Bayeux was in the capable hands of Matthew Gough, and his men held out valiantly, driving off two impetuous, and unauthorised, French attempts in the same day attempting to take advantage of the breaches in the walls to take the town by assault. Nevertheless, it was clear that when the French launched a properly coordinated assault there would be little hope for the garrison. Gough elected to negotiate the surrender of the town. There were around 900 English in the town, between 300 and 400 of whom were women, as well as many children. All were authorised to go to Cherbourg, although the men were not allowed to take their arms, had to leave on foot, and were required to carry a wooden staff as a sign that they were unarmed. The French, seeing the pitiful sate of the population, allowed women of rank to leave on horseback. They also provided horse-drawn carts for children and other women.[26]

Four days before Bayeux fell, Avranches with its garrison of between 400 and 500 men, surrendered to the combined forces of the Duke of Brittany and Richemont after three weeks of siege, skirmishing, and heavy bombardment. The terms of surrender were much as at Bayeux with the garrison leaving on foot with a wooden staff. The two most important towns still in English hands were Caen and Cherbourg.

Before turning their attention to these latter two towns, during May the French took several other smaller towns and fortresses. Tombelaine is an island in the estuary of the Sélune. It is about one-and-a-half miles north of Mont-Saint-Michel, and only being accessible at low tide, would be out of range of artillery fire. It was reputed to be virtually impregnable if properly provisioned. However, the English garrison of around 80 or 90 men appear to have had no stomach for a fight when they saw the size of the host arrayed against them, although perhaps the 500 *écus* offered to the captain of the garrison helped him make his decision. The garrison surrendered and marched for Cherbourg, once again leaving the valuable

---

25   Barker, *Conquest, The English Kingdom of France*, p.396. Nicolle, *The Fall of English France*, p.38. Chartier, *Chronique de Charles VII, Roi de* France, vol.2, pp.201–2. Monstrelet, *Chroniques*, vol.10, p.258.

26   Barker, *Conquest, The English Kingdom of France*, pp.395–6. Nicolle, *The Fall of English France*, pp.29–35. Chartier, *Chronique de Charles VII, Roi de* France, vol. 2, pp.204–207.

THE RECONQUEST OF NORMANDY 1449-50

artillery in French hands.[27] The two towns of Bricquebec and Valognes, the latter having been garrisoned by about 120 men since its fall to the English in April, both surrendered, and their garrisons joined the ever-growing procession of English troops heading for Cherbourg.

In early June Jacques de Luxembourg was despatched with an advanced party of around 200 men to lay siege to the town and castle of Saint-Sauveur-le-Vicomte in the Cotentin peninsula, about 18 miles south of Cherbourg. He was subsequently joined by men from the Breton and French armies and trenches were opened for the siege. There seem to have been no cannon present, with all available artillery being gathered for the siege of Caen. Nevertheless, the 200 men holding the town and castle preferred to surrender. They were given seven days to evacuate the town and castle, which were then handed over to the French.[28]

The French now concentrated their forces for the key target of Caen. On 5 June 1450, the siege force gathered. The Constable, de Richemont, arrived south-west of the town near the Abbey of Saint-Étienne. He was joined by Clermont and together they were reported to have had 1,200 lances (7,200 men), between 4,000 and 5,000 other mounted troops, including archers, and 2,000 *franc-archers*. Dunois set up his camp to the south-east in the suburb of Vaucelles. He had with him 500 lances (3,000 men), 2,500 mounted troops including archers, and 2,000 *franc-archers*. The besieging force exceeded 20,000 men, while inside Caen were said to be 4,000 English. The proportion of combatants is not known, but in normal times a garrison of that size could be expected, if well supplied and with sound defensive works, to put up a robust defence for some time until relief arrived. However, these were not normal times.

There was no realistic prospect of relief, and the English were going to be subjected to the mining expertise and artillery of Jean Bureau. Bureau mustered the artillery in preparation for the bombardment and drafted in labourers, miners, and carpenters to dig mines running into the ditches surrounding the town. The mining and artillery bombardment rapidly took effect, and several breaches were made in the walls. To add to the problems of the garrison, at some point Charles VII arrived with a further 600 lances (3,600 men) and a body of archers. There were numerous skirmishes between the besieging troops and the garrison with losses on both sides but with no advantage to either the French or English. However after three weeks it was clear to Somerset that it was only a matter of time before the town and castle would be taken by assault. The loss of life would probably have been heavy on both sides. It was thus in the interest of everyone that a composition should be reached for the surrender of Caen.

On 25 June 1450, Somerset put his seal to the surrender document. For the sake of form, time was given for the arrival of a relief force, which

---

27   Monstrelet, *Chroniques*, vol.10, p.260.
28   Nicolle, *The Fall of English France*, pp.38 & 41. Chartier, *Chronique de Charles VII, Roi de* France, vol.2, pp.202–204 and 211–212.

THE BATTLE OF CASTILLON 1453

both French and English would have known was impossible. The date of surrender was set as 1 July, and it was agreed that there would be a truce pending the surrender. Somerset agreed to pay 300,000 *écus* in reparations to Charles VII for his costs and damage incurred to the town and castle. Twelve Englishmen, six Norman knights in English service and four burghers were handed over to the French as hostages to guarantee the terms of the surrender. On the due date the occupants would be allowed to leave with their possessions provided that all debts had been settled. They would be permitted to take personal possessions with them but all artillery, archery stores, and crossbows were to be left behind.

On this occasion there could be no question of the garrison leaving to reinforce the handful of remaining English held strongholds. They would be escorted to the port of Ouistreham, nine miles north-west of Caen for direct passage to England, although some including Somerset and his family, probably fearing his reception in England having surrendered an important town for the second time in eight months, were escorted to Calais.

Caen Castle. (Peter Hoskins)

Indeed, apparently aware of the enormity of his failure to hold Caen, it seems that he offered Robin Campbell, lieutenant of Charles VII's Scots Guard, 4,000 *écus* to kidnap leading French commanders, including Dunois, and lead 1,500 men out of Caen. They would then seize Charles VII and take him to Cherbourg. The French gunpowder store would be set alight, and guns spiked. The plot, if it was ever realistic, came to nothing, and was only discovered some years later, but the delay did not save Campbell who was executed for treason. On 1 July, the town and castle were surrendered, the hostages released and those who wished to do so left Caen. On 6 July Charles VII made a ceremonial entry into the town.[29]

The only places of importance remaining in English hands were Falaise, 20 miles south of Caen, Domfort, 40 miles south-west of Caen, and Cherbourg on the northern tip of the Cotentin peninsula. On 6 July, the day that Charles VII entered Caen, Poton de Xaintrailles arrived to lay

---

29   Barker, *Conquest, The English Kingdom of France*, pp.397–8. Nicolle, *The Fall of English France*, pp.38–9. Chartier, *Chronique de Charles VII, Roi de France*, vol.2, pp.214–21. Basin, *Histoire de Charles VII et Louis XI*, pp.260–63. Monstrelet, *Chroniques*, vol.10, pp.274–85.

siege to Falaise; two days later Jean Bureau arrived with *franc-archers* and artillery. Part of the garrison sallied out to try to seize the artillery train but were driven off and returned to the safety of the town. Although the garrison was some 1,500 strong, they quickly concluded that in the face of the strength of the artillery being deployed they had little hope of holding out. On 10 July, a composition was agreed for the surrender of the town and castle. Once again, for the sake of form, time was allowed for the arrival of a relief force, which both sides must have known was extremely improbable, and the surrender was set for 21 July. In addition to the standard agreement for the garrison to depart with safe conduct, the captain secured the release of John Talbot, the Earl of Shrewsbury, who was being held in the castle at Dreux. Shrewsbury had been handed over as a guarantor of the terms of surrender of Rouen, including the surrender of Harfleur. Because Harfleur had initially refused to surrender, he was still in French hands. Since the town had subsequently fallen to the French, releasing him was a small price to pay for the surrender of Falaise. On 21 July, Falaise was handed over to the French.

The French now moved on to Domfront, defended by 700 to 800 men. Only two days after the fall of Falaise, 23 July, Jean Bureau arrived with his artillery, 1,500 *franc-archers* and an unknown number of men-at-arms. The garrison quickly came to the same conclusion as that of Falaise and agreed a composition to surrender the town on 2 August to return to England, with the usual provision of leaving with their goods.[30]

All that remained to complete the reconquest of Normandy was to take Cherbourg. This was a formidable fortress that had never been taken by assault since the construction of its defences a century before. It was built on a narrow spit of rock, surrounded by three concentric walls, and also protected by the sea, which turned the fortress into an island at high tide. It could hold a garrison of a thousand men, and it had the advantage that it could be resupplied by sea from England. In June the garrison had received supplies of saltpetre and sulphur for gunpowder manufacture, bows, arrows, bowstrings, wheat, malt, and hops. It had held out as an English outpost for 16 years in the late fourteenth century and it had taken five months for Gloucester to take it in 1418, and then it only fell only with the help of a traitor in the garrison. If ever a fortress could have been expected to hold out, then this was it.

The Constable of France, Arthur de Richemont, had opened the siege on 6 July. With the fall of Falaise and Domfront Jean Bureau was able to redeploy his artillery to Cherbourg. Bureau was undeterred by the problem of the tide and deployed guns on the sands. They were covered with waxed hides weighed down by stones and wooden beams when the tide came in and uncovered when the tide went out. With the other guns deployed on firm ground he was able to maintain a bombardment from all sides. The bombardment was not without incident with four French guns

---

30   Chartier, *Chronique de Charles VII, Roi de* France, vol.2, pp.223–8.

exploding during use, a not uncommon occurrence. The garrison was also well equipped with artillery and casualties were suffered by both sides. Nevertheless, the captain of Cherbourg, Thomas Gower, decided that the situation was hopeless and started negotiations for surrender. On 12 August, terms were agreed for the handing over the town and castle on 22 August. Once again, in England the government took measures that were too late to be of help. Two days after the agreement to surrender, authorisation was given to seize shipping to go to the aid of Cherbourg. When news reached England of the surrender of the town, the captain was seen as something of a hero for having held out longer than many other places. What the public did not know was that he had in effect sold the fortress to the French. Gower's son Richard, like Shrewsbury a hostage since the capitulation of Rouen, was released without ransom, 2,000 *écus* were paid to the garrison, a similar sum was paid to discharge other prisoners of their ransoms, all expenses for returning the English and their possessions to England were paid by the French, and unspecified secret gifts were given to unnamed members of the garrison.[31]

In a little over a year the English had been expelled from Normandy after more than 30 years in possession.

There were many reasons for this rapid disintegration of English power. There had been a fundamental difference of perception between the English and the French concerning the Truce of Tours. Henry VI laboured under the illusion that Charles VII shared his wish for a peaceful end to the war, which would leave Normandy as an English possession. Charles VII prepared for a return to war, reforming his armies, investing in artillery, and building up a war chest. Meanwhile Henry VI, despite warnings as early as 1445 from the Duke of Suffolk that garrisons should be maintained and victuals and arms replenished, allowed the English military capability to decline. In the background to this lack of preparation was the reality that Normandy, in contrast to the Calais Pale that was of economic value to England, was a drain on resources. War weariness had set in, and as the years went by, there was increasing reluctance to raise taxes to fund defence in the duchy. When those back in England woke up to the situation, measures taken were too little too late. In addition to the lack of preparedness in towns and fortresses there was no field army, which could offer relief for a besieged garrison. Once towns and castles started to fall, the strength of the reformed French armies and the effectiveness of their artillery were evident to all. Towns and castles could be expected to hold out for a considerable time if well supplied, but with no realistic hope of relief it was much better to make a favourable settlement than risk losing everything if the place were taken by assault. Many of the English had married and raised families in Normandy, not only did they risk losing their freedom or their lives but also their personal wealth and families. This must have weighed in the calculations of many,

---

31   Barker, *Conquest, The English Kingdom of France*, pp.398–400. Chartier, *Chronique de Charles VII, Roi de* France, vol.2, pp.231–234.

and as the news of the collapse spread, morale must have been steadily eroded. It is impossible to say how important each factor was in the fall of towns and fortresses, although the effect of the artillery often appears in the contemporary accounts. What is clear is that the time for which places held out was much shorter than had been the case in earlier phases of the war.[32]

Now that Normandy had fallen Charles could focus all his efforts on Gascony. He wasted no time in doing so, with the campaign in Gascony opening only two months after the fall of Cherbourg.

---

32   Peter Hoskins, *Siege Warfare During the Hundred Years' War* (Barnsley: Pen & Sword, 2018), pp.214–217.

6

The French Conquest of Gascony: The First Campaign

While the main focus of the war since the collapse of the Truce of Tours had been in Normandy, there had also been fighting in Gascony, with two small castles at Saint-Thomas-de-Conac and Saint-Maigrin (20 miles apart and about 45 miles north of Bordeaux) falling to the French in May 1449, two months before the formal end of the truce. The capture of these two places had been with the connivance of the Duke of Brittany, probably with the objective of putting pressure on the English to return Fougères.[1]

The Count of Foix, Gaston IV, had allied himself with Charles VII. Towards the end of the summer of 1449, he laid siege to Mauléon-Licharre, 35 miles south-east of the major English held town of Bayonne, in the Basque Country close to the Pyrenees. He is said to have an army of 600 men-at-arms, between 10,000 and 12,000 infantry, and an artillery train. Accounts of the siege vary. One version recounts that the townspeople quickly took fright at the prospect of the town falling to Foix by assault and agreed a composition. In return for their lives and property being guaranteed they would hand over the town. The Anglo-Gascon garrison then withdrew into the castle, which was said to be very strong with a high tower standing on rock. The Count of Foix was undeterred, knowing that the garrison was small and that supplies were in short supply.

An alternative narrative is that siege was laid to the town and castle together. The King of Navarre had learned what was afoot and marched towards Mauléon with 6,000 men to relieve the siege. As he approached the town, he appreciated that he faced a much larger force that had also prepared defences for its position. He halted his army about five miles away and opened negotiations with de Foix. Navarre pointed out that he was responsible to King Henry VI of England for the safekeeping of the town and castle. Gaston, his son-in-law, replied that he was Charles VII's

---

1   Chartier, *Chronique de Charles VII, Roi de* France, vol.2, pp.74–75.

THE FRENCH CONQUEST OF GASCONY: THE FIRST CAMPAIGN

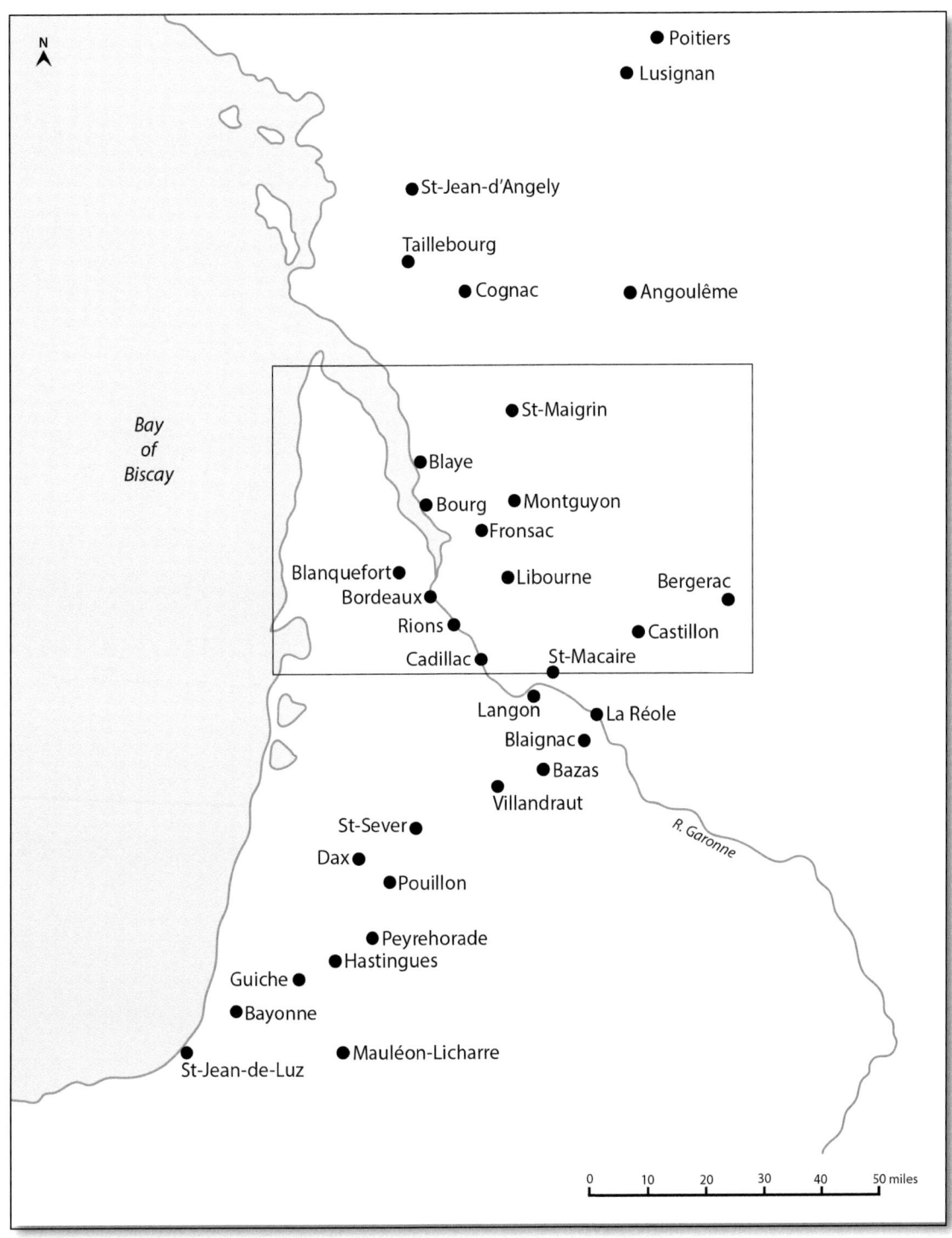

The French conquest of Gascony, 1450–53

THE BATTLE OF CASTILLON 1453

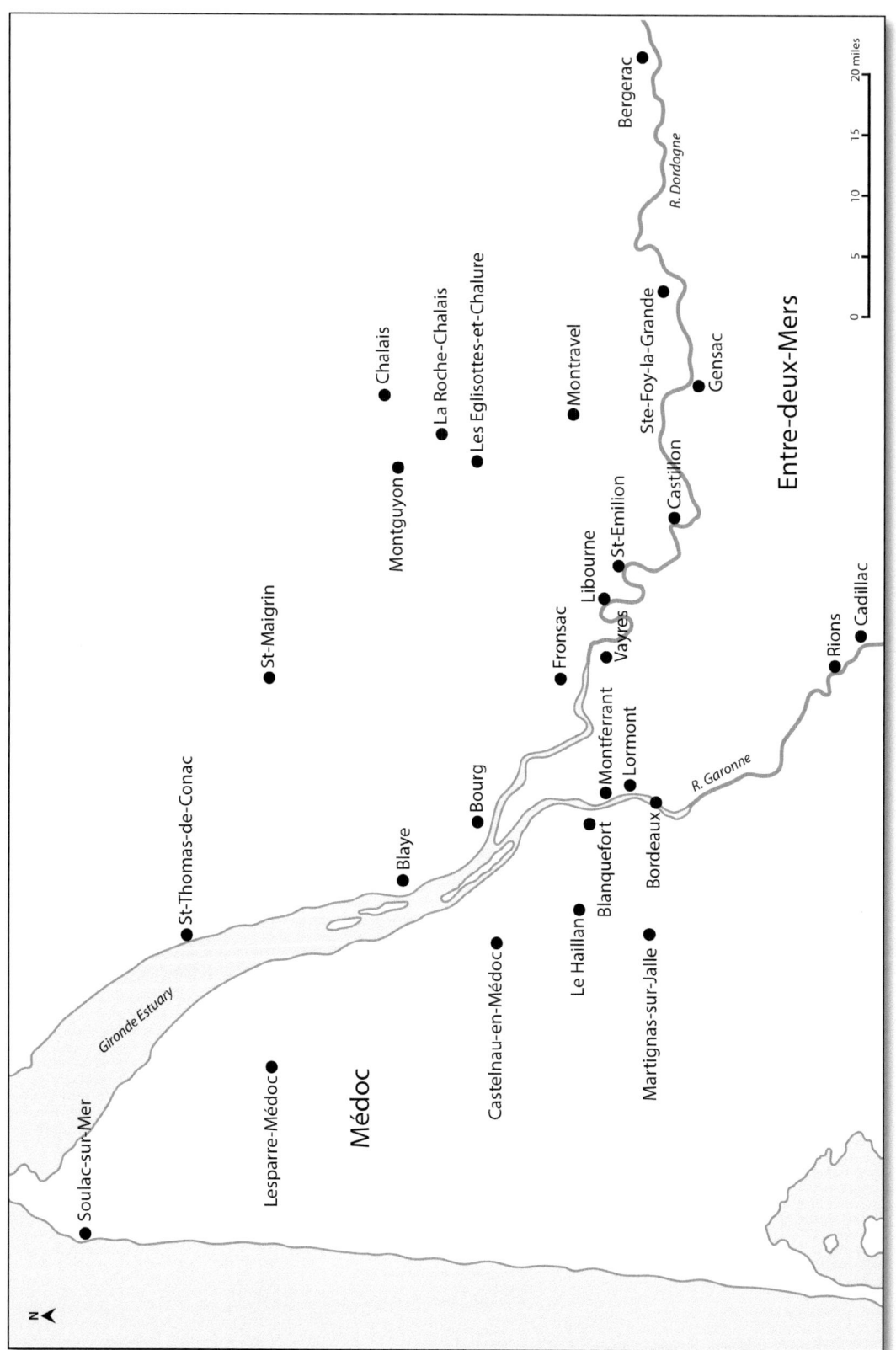

The French conquest of Gascony, the Bordeaux Region, 1450–53

lieutenant-general for the lands between the river Gironde and the Pyrenees and had been ordered to take Mauléon. He would not in any circumstances, other than if defeated, give up the siege.

Navarre was heavily outnumbered, and it is also likely that he wanted to avoid war with his son-in-law – he withdrew leaving the garrison to its fate. With all hope of relief gone the garrison of Mauléon-Licharre agreed a treaty of surrender during the early part of September. The exact circumstances of the surrender are unclear. However, it seems that it was not the unfavourable military situation that led to the surrender but rather the treachery of the captain of the garrison, Luis de Beaumont, whose lordships in Gascony were subsequently confiscated by King Henry VI:

> …the lands, lordships and possessions which Luis de Beaumont, called the alférez of Navarre, had in the Aquitaine and elsewhere in the King's realm and lordships, were confiscated into the King's hands, because Beaumont committed the crime of lèse-majesté, as is well known, because he treacherously handed over the King's town and castle of Mauléon to the King's adversarie.[2]

Whatever the truth of the matter, there seems to have been considerable fighting and bombardment with losses on both sides and in such circumstances, where a garrison surrendered, the terms granted were normally less favourable than those agreed when the surrender was made early in a siege. This proved to be the case in this instance. The garrison asked to be allowed to depart with their arms and possessions. This was refused, and they left without horses, arms, or possessions. They were permitted to leave with a wooden stick and one silver coin worth ten pence to pay for food and water on their route to safety.[3]

The next move by Foix was to seize the small town and castle of Guiche, 15 miles to the east of Bayonne. It is generally recorded that the move to take Guiche took place in February 1450, however, the surrender document is dated 15 December 1449.[4] Although the precise start date of the siege of Guiche is unrecorded, it is logical to think that, having mustered his army, Gaston IV would have moved on to Guiche immediately from Mauléon. His force was equipped with artillery and he set about undermining and bombarding the walls. The garrison, which is recorded as being between 700 and 800 strong (an improbably high number in view of the small size of the castle), made sorties to disrupt the besiegers and there were casualties on both sides. The garrison sent for help to the English in Bayonne and Dax,

---

2   Guillaume Leseur (Henri Courteault ed.), *Histoire de Gaston IV, Comte de Foix*, vol.1 (Paris: Renouard, 1893), p.65, n.1. Gascon Rolls, gasconrolls.org, C61/40, Membrane 9–4.
3   Chartier, *Chronique de Charles VII, Roi de France*, vol.2, pp.127–130. Leseur, *Histoire de Gaston IV*, vol.1, pp.47–67.
4   Leseur, *Histoire de Gaston IV*, vol.1 (Paris: Renouard, vol.1 1893), p.94, n.1.

16 miles north-east. The Constable of Navarre and the Mayor of Bayonne led a force, probably around 3,000 strong, in an attempt to relieve the town. They approached Guiche by boat along the river Adour, which runs about a mile below the castle. However, after disembarking, they were ambushed by the besieging force, and most of the Anglo-Gascon force was driven off, but with some taking refuge in the castle. With all hope for relief now gone, the garrison surrendered the next morning. Once again, de Foix allowed the men to depart, but without arms and possessions and carrying a wooden stave.[5]

Following the surrender of Guiche, 15 or 16 other fortresses were taken or handed over, including Hastingues, Pouillon and Peyrehorade. By May 1450, it seems that Saint-Jean-de-Luz and the lands of Labourd had also fallen into the hands of Gaston IV.[6] Labourd bordered on Bayonne and Gaston had now a string of fortresses and towns from the coast of the Bay of Biscay inland along the Adour and beyond for 25 miles. He was well placed to move north from the south of English Gascony when the time was right.

It would have been reasonable to think that the conquest of Gascony would be a harder task than that of Normandy. Although the English suffered from long lines of communication from ports such as Portsmouth and Plymouth to Bordeaux, they had been involved in the Duchy of Aquitaine ever since the marriage of Eleanor of Aquitaine to Henry Plantagenet (King Henry II of England from 1154) three centuries before, in 1152. Over the centuries there had been an ebb and flow of the borders of English held Gascony and the allegiances of noble families. However, many noble families had been consistently loyal to the Kings of England in their capacity as Dukes of Aquitaine. Among the bourgeoisie and merchant classes there were strong economic interests for maintaining ties with England, so much so that during the reign of Edward III the municipal officers of Saint-Émilion petitioned the King to the effect that they should remain annexed to the English crown in perpetuity.[7] Although there had been an important involvement of English administrators there had been no colonisation, and high office was often held by Gascons. In the event, as we shall see, in in less than a year the French had seemingly completed the conquest with the great city of Bordeaux in their hands. However, as we shall also see, the underlying ties between the Gascons and the English meant that this was not the end of the story.

In September 1450, after the victory in Normandy, Charles VII called his commanders together at Tours. Also present was the immensely rich merchant Jacques Coeur, who had provided much of the money for the conquest of Normandy. He undertook again to raise money for the forthcoming campaign. Charles VII appointed Jean de Blois, Count of Penthièvre, to command the army to start the conquest of Gascony. The

---

5 Chartier, *Chronique de Charles VII, Roi de* France, vol.2, pp.186–187. Leseur, *Histoire de Gaston IV*, vol.1, pp.69–95.
6 Leseur, *Histoire de Gaston IV*, vol.1, pp.96–105.
7 D, Brissaud, *Les Anglais en Guyenne* (Paris: J.-B. Dumoulin, 1875), p.247.

THE FRENCH CONQUEST OF GASCONY: THE FIRST CAMPAIGN

army was composed of 500 to 600 lances (3,000 to 3,600 men) and an unknown number of archers; Jean Bureau brought the artillery. The first target was Bergerac on the river Dordogne, 50 miles east of Bordeaux.

Penthièvre was in charge of the siege, and faced with superior forces and bombardment by Bureau's artillery Bergerac's captain agreed a composition. The town was surrendered on 10 October 1450 and the garrison were allowed to leave with their horses and possessions. The French left a garrison in Bergerac and then moved down the Dordogne, and the small castle of Gensac towards Castillon was taken by assault. The French suffered a handful of casualties and 25 to 30 of the garrison are reported as being killed, with the remainder taken prisoner.[8]

The army now split into two. One part took Sainte-Foy-la-Grande, which surrendered on the mere approach of the French, and the other part of the army took La-Roche-Chalais, 30 miles to the north, and the castle of Monfourat in Les-Églisottes-et-Chalaure, six miles south-west of La-Roche-Chalais. In both cases, the surrender was negotiated after a short siege.[9] The second part of the army marched south-west 35 miles to Bazas, which surrendered on 31 October. At the beginning of November, the Lord of Orval marched north from Bazas into the Médoc just north of Bordeaux, near the town of Blanquefort. He only had 400 to 500 men with him, and it is likely that his objective was limited to reconnaissance and the harrying of the countryside outside the major towns. The English Mayor of Bordeaux, Gadifer Shorthouse, sallied out of Bordeaux with a motley force of men-at-arms and ill-trained and ill-equipped town militia. French sources put this force at some 8,000 to 10,000 men. Orval routed this ill-disciplined and disorganised Anglo-Gascon force when they were near Le Haillan, only five miles from Bordeaux's walls, with reports of up to 1,800 killed and 1,200 prisoners taken. These figures seem improbably high, but, whatever the figures for the relative strengths of the forces engaged and the losses sustained, this was a serious and potentially hazardous setback for Bordeaux. Orval wanted to seize the opportunity but needed reinforcements. He sent messengers to the King at Montbazon asking for 300 lances to allow him to follow up his success. The first reaction of Charles VII was to support the request, but then news came that Orval had been forced to withdraw in the face of a hostile population. In addition, the French fleet that was planned to support the campaign on the Gironde had not yet been assembled, the

---

8   The chronicler Chartier, *Chronique de Charles VII, Roi de* France, vol.2, p.241 and n.1, calls this place either Jansac or Jonsac. Several historians have interpreted this as being the town of Jonzac. This makes little sense, Jonzac is 50 miles away to the north-west. Also, Chartier records that Jansac/Jonsac was on the Dordogne, which corresponds with Gensac.
9   Chartier, *Chronique de Charles VII, Roi de* France, vol.2, pp.237–243. Fresne de Beaucourt, *Histoire de Charles VII*, vol.5, pp.40–43. Chartier records that the second castle was called Montferrand and some have interpreted this as Monferrand-du-Périgord, 20 miles south-east of Bergerac. Fresne de Beaucourt (p.43, n.4.) argues for Montfourat; this makes more sense geographically.

necessary funds not having been collected, and winter was approaching. After sober reflection, it seemed unlikely that 300 extra lances would be sufficient to drive the Anglo-Gascons from Bordeaux and their other strongholds. Under these circumstances Charles VII decided to suspend operations until the spring.[10]

With the coming of spring the French were ready to resume operations. At the end of March, the King was in Tours, and on 31 March he appointed the Count of Dunois as his lieutenant-general to conquer Gascony. Dunois had with him Jean Bureau and his artillery and the Count of Angoulême, and the army numbered up to 400 lances, infantry and 3,000 *franc-archers*, probably more than 6,000 men in total. The first target was Montguyon, 30 miles north-east of Bordeaux. The castle was besieged from 28 April and a surrender document was signed on 6 May. Five days were given for a relief force to arrive, and four hostages were given up as guarantors of the terms of the agreement. When relief did not arrive, the castle was surrendered on 11 May 1451. The hostages were released, and the garrison marched out with all their possessions, except for the artillery which was left in place. Those who wished to remain and swear allegiance to Charles VII were permitted to do so. The French provided horses and wagons to transport possessions to Libourne, under the agreement that the wagons would be returned.[11]

Four days after the surrender of Montguyon, Dunois arrived before Blaye, on the right bank of the river Gironde, reputed to be the strongest place in Anglo-Gascon hands after Bordeaux. The French army continued to grow with the arrival of fresh contingents composed of more men-at-arms and archers. During the winter, the planned fleet had also been gathered and this arrived off Blaye bringing supplies for the army. The Anglo-Gascons had also sent five ships from Bordeaux to support the garrison in Blaye. These were scattered by the French fleet and driven back to Bordeaux, freeing the French ships to blockade Blaye from the river side. To increase the pressure on the garrison the Count of Penthièvre arrived with further men. Trenches and mines were dug, and Bureau began to bombard the walls, which were breached in several places, then on 20 May an assault was launched. Two hundred of the garrison are reported as either killed or captured, with the remainder withdrawing into the castle. Faced with overwhelming force and with no hope of relief reaching them either by river or overland the garrison surrendered on 24 May 1451. The surrender terms were very much in line with those of other towns, but with two added terms: all silver was to be left and the members of the garrison who left had to give their word not to take up arms again against Charles VII during the next four months.[12]

---

10 Chartier, *Chronique de Charles VII, Roi de* France, vol.2, pp.246–249. Fresne de Beaucourt, *Histoire de Charles VII*, vol.5, pp.43–45.
11 Chartier, *Chronique de Charles VII, Roi de* France, vol. 2, pp.249–253. Fresne de Beaucourt, *Histoire de Charles VII*, vol.5, pp.45–46.
12 Chartier, *Chronique de Charles VII, Roi de* France, vol.2, pp.254–249, Fresne de Beaucourt, *Histoire de Charles VII*, vol.5, p.46.

THE FRENCH CONQUEST OF GASCONY: THE FIRST CAMPAIGN

From Blaye the fleet and the army moved eight miles up the Gironde to besiege the town and castle of Bourg, also on the right bank. The 400 or 500 strong garrison found themselves in a similar position to those at Blaye a few days before, cut off from relief either by river or by land and surrounded by vastly superior forces well equipped with artillery. After four days the garrison had had enough, and it surrendered on 29 May.[13]

Bourg stands at the confluence of the Garonne and Dordogne, which then become the Gironde. With Bourg in their hands the French controlled access by water up the Dordogne to Libourne, Saint-Émilion and Castillon. Within the next few days, several places surrendered: Libourne opened its gates without resistance on 30 May and Castillon, which had been besieged by the Count of Penthièvre after the fall of Blaye, surrendered the same day. Saint-Émilion preferred to avoid a siege and opened its gates to the French on 5 June. The strong fortress of Fronsac, just outside Libourne, had been besieged from 2 June, but on 5 June the garrison, having for the sake of form and honour been given ten days to wait for an improbable relief, undertook to surrender on 15 June if the besieging forces had not been driven off by a relieving army. On 14 June the French army was arrayed for battle. Unsurprisingly, there was no sign of relief and the garrison handed over the castle the following day. The surrender of Fronsac also committed the Anglo-Gascons to hand over Vaiyres on the Dordogne, Rions and Saint-Macaire on the Garonne, and Blaignac just south of La Réole on the Garonne.[14]

With the French fleet in control of the Gironde, and their armies having garrisoned strong places on the Garonne and the Dordogne, Bordeaux was in a precarious position. However, while all this had been going on attention was also turning to the south of Gascony at Dax, 80 miles southwest of Bordeaux. The Count of Foix had started preparing for the siege of Dax in February and had received help from Charles VII. He had also received financial assistance to fund his army from Jacques Coeur. The operation was to include men from the main army further north, and it was these who arrived first, with 300 lances and 2,000 crossbowmen led by the Lord of Albret. The Count of Foix was not far behind, arriving only a matter of hours later with 500 lances and an additional 2,000 crossbowmen. However, despite the size of the besieging army, and the presence of both stone-throwing and gunpowder artillery, the town held out. It was only after the capitulation of Bordeaux on 23 June 1451 that Dax had little choice but to surrender.[15]

---

13 Chartier, *Chronique de Charles VII, Roi de* France, vol.2, pp.261–264. Fresne de Beaucourt, *Histoire de Charles VII*, vol.5, p.46.
14 Chartier, *Chronique de Charles VII, Roi de* France, vol.2, pp.266–75. Fresne de Beaucourt, *Histoire de Charles VII*, vol.5, p.46 & pp.213–5.
15 Chartier, *Chronique de Charles VII, Roi de* France, vol.2, pp.265–6. Henry Ribadieu, *Histoire de la Conquête de la Guyenne par les Français, de ses Antécédents et ses Suits*, (Bordeaux: Paul Chaumas, 1866), pp.219–220 & 255. Leseur, *Histoire de Gaston IV*, vol.1, pp.115–122.

After the capitulation of Fronsac, the French turned their attention to Bordeaux. Despite the arrival of reinforcements from the garrisons of other towns and fortresses which had surrendered, and the willingness of the nobility whose families had long been loyal to the English Crown to resist, it was evident that the town was in a parlous position. Messengers are said to have been sent to England to call for help, although this seems unlikely since the French held Bourg and Blaye on the Gironde and had ships in the river blocking the approaches to Bordeaux. There were also rumours of reinforcements already being on their way by sea. However, after some sporadic acts of resistance, the leaders of the town recognised the hopeless situation that they faced against a large army including Bureau's artillery, and with no realistic hope of immediate help from England. On 12 June 1451, a treaty of capitulation was signed. The terms were generous; the inhabitants were given a delay until 23 June for the arrival of a relief force; the confrontation between any relief force and the French army was set to be near Fronsac. If a relief force was not forthcoming the gates of Bordeaux would be opened to the French on 24 June. In addition, all other towns, castles, and fortresses were to be delivered up to the French – hence the surrender of Dax above.

It must have been clear to everyone that the English were not going to come to the rescue, but at least honour was saved. In the unlikely event of an English army arriving and carrying the day the French would return the recently acquired towns and fortresses of Vayres, Blaignac, Castillon, Rions and Saint-Macaire. Inhabitants throughout Gascony who swore allegiance to the King of France would keep all privileges previously granted to them. Furthermore, it was agreed that the inhabitants of Gascony would only contribute taxes and men for the King of France's service with their agreement. Those who did not wish to swear allegiance to the King were free to leave and had six months to arrange their affairs. They could take with them all their possessions, merchandise, ships, gold, and silver. An amnesty was granted for any criminal and civil prosecutions, so that those who wished to go would not be encumbered by legal proceedings. With the fall of Bordeaux Jean Bureau was appointed as mayor.[16]

Of the principal Gascon nobles, Gaston de Foix-Grailly, the Captal de Buch, and his son Jean, Viscount of Castillon and Earl of Kendal, declined to swear allegiance to Charles VII. Their family had long been loyal to the Kings of England, and both had been admitted as members of the Order of the Garter during Henry VI's reign. Once again Charles VII was generous; if they chose to go into exile, they could retain all their properties which had come into their possession by inheritance or granted to their family by the Kings of England. These possessions could also pass to their descendants, on condition that those descendants swore allegiance to the French

---

16   Chartier, *Chronique de Charles VII, Roi de* France, vol.2, pp.277–291. Ribadieu, *Histoire de la Conquête de la Guyenne par les Français,* pp.214–237. Fresne de Beaucourt, *Histoire de Charles VII*, vol.5, pp.47–51.

THE FRENCH CONQUEST OF GASCONY: THE FIRST CAMPAIGN

crown. There was also a supplementary secret agreement whereby the King of France would pay the capital de Buch 15,000 *écus* when Bordeaux surrendered. With these provisions, Charles VII astutely avoided immediate problems with the Foix-Graillys and ensured the family's allegiance in the future. Gaston de Foix-Grailly decided to sell his lands in Gascony to his nephew Gaston IV, Count of Foix, for 84,000 *écus*, and withdrew to his lands at Maella in Aragon. He never returned to Gascony and died in exile a few years later. His son went to England in 1451 but returned to Gascony for the subsequent campaign.[17]

With Bordeaux in French hands the only remaining stronghold was Bayonne on the coast in the far south of Gascony. In principle it should have been handed over to Charles VII after the surrender of Bordeaux, since the treaty signed by the Estates of Bordeaux required them to: '…deliver to the King of France the town of Bordeaux and with it the other towns, castles and fortresses of Gascony and the Bordelais.' A herald was sent to Bayonne by Dunois with a copy of the treaty demanding that the town surrender. The herald received short shrift and was sent packing. It was thus clear to the French that Bayonne would have to be taken by force.[18]

From July to September Charles VII was at the castle of Taillebourg, 70 miles north of Bordeaux, and it was here that he held a council to prepare plans for the capture of Bayonne. The commanders were to be the Counts of Dunois and Foix. Gaston IV had mustered 300 lances and an unspecified number of archers and infantry. Dunois had with him 800 lances. Gaspard Bureau was commander of the artillery. They would undoubtedly have been accompanied by archers, *franc-archers*, and infantry but we do not have numbers. The Count of Foix set up his siege camp near the suburb of Saint-Léon to the south of the town, while the Dunois established his camp between the rivers Nive, which ran through the centre of the town, and the Adour to the east. If the town were to be completely surrounded and besieged then there was no option but to place men between the two rivers,

Taillebourg castle stands on high ground overlooking the river Charente. It was closely associated with Anglo-French rivalry. Eleanor of Aquitaine and her first husband Louis VII stayed here on the night of their marriage, Eleanor's son, Richard I, captured the castle in 1179, and in July 1242 the army of Henry III was driven off by Louis IX before the French victory outside Saintes two days later. It was used by Charles VII as his headquarters in the summer of 1451 after the fall of Bordeaux, to plan the capture of Bayonne. The castle was rebuilt in 1423; the only structure remaining from this period is a tower.

---

17 Matthieu Nicolas, *La Dynastie des Grailly : une famille noble au cœur de la guerre de Cent Ans* (Toulouse: University Toulouse Jean Jaurès, 2017), pp.52 and 57, Chartier, *Chronique de Charles VII, Roi de* France, vol.2, pp.291–298. Supplementary information from Guilhem Pépin.
18 Ribadieu, *Histoire de la Conquête de la Guyenne par les Français*, pp.228 and 255.

although this had the potential to hinder mutual support between the two contingents.

The suburb of Saint-Léon was well protected by deep ditches, wooden palisades, and artillery. However, in the face of the strength of the gathering besieging force, and after a French assault which had cost the garrison 60 killed, the following morning the garrison commanders decided to abandon the suburb and retire within the town, taking their artillery with them. As they withdrew, they set light to houses and churches – no doubt, as was common practice, to deny their use to the attackers for either shelter or protection. The French tried to pursue the retiring troops into the town but without scaling ladders were unable to cross the deep ditches and palisades. However, they did extinguish the fires and Foix set up his headquarters within the suburb, in the Augustinian monastery.

Around 12 August, the Lord of Albret and the Viscount of Tartras arrived with a further 200 lances, an unknown number of archers, and 3,000 crossbowmen. Over the next few days there were sorties by the garrison and skirmishes with the besiegers, and it became apparent to Dunois that an assault was likely to be extremely costly unless breaches were opened in the walls. The garrison watched the preparations, with mines approaching the walls and the first breaches from artillery fire appearing. Having seen the arrival of 12 ships bringing supplies and more men, which also ended the hope of support coming by sea, the garrison must have been aware that there was no prospect of relief and that their position would become increasingly desperate. The defenders therefore asked for talks to negotiate a surrender. There is some doubt over the date of the decision: some sources state this occurred on 18 August, but others relate it to a story that on 20 August at 7.00 a.m. a white cross was seen in the sky (that of St Denis, patron Saint of the French Monarchy), which convinced the defenders that God was on the side of the French.

Whatever the date, the negotiations progressed rapidly. The terms were harsher than had become usual, perhaps because of the resistance in defiance of the treaty for the surrender signed at Bordeaux. The governor of Bayonne, Jean de Beaumont, was to surrender immediately as a guarantor of the terms of the agreement to hand over the town on 21 August. Merchants and other prisoners could either remain and swear allegiance to the French Crown, or they were to leave for England within six months taking all their possessions with them.[19] All the garrison would be treated as prisoners at the mercy of the King and his commanders, forfeiting all their possessions. Once the surrender was formally made the prisoners were granted clemency and freed; they were permitted to retain their property against a payment to Charles VII of 40,000 *écus*. Later in the year Charles VII returned half of the indemnity as a sign of clemency to his new subjects.

---

19   Monstrelet, *Chroniques*, vol.10, p.315.

THE FRENCH CONQUEST OF GASCONY: THE FIRST CAMPAIGN

Bayonne had been in the hands of the English since the marriage of Eleanor of Aquitaine, Duchess of Aquitaine, to Henry Plantagenet in 1152.[20] After almost three centuries it passed to France and its surrender seemed to signal the end of the English involvement in Gascony. Bourg, Blaye and Bordeaux were garrisoned by the French and senior appointments made for the government of Gascony. But there was a final act still to come.

Elsewhere in France, the only remaining English holding was Calais, an important foothold not only symbolically and militarily but also commercially. There had been concern in England that the French would attempt to take the town after the fall of Normandy. With the defeat in Gascony this concern became more acute. There were even fears of a French invasion of England, and the Duke of Somerset was appointed to the captaincy of Calais. He immediately began reinforcing the town and 500 men and 12 ships were sent across the Channel during August.

On the French side counter rumours were running that the English would send three armies to land in Calais, Brittany, and Normandy. It seems that Charles VII did indeed have the intention of attempting the taking of Calais once the campaigning season started anew in 1452. In the event this all came to nothing. John Talbot, Earl of Shrewsbury had been appointed on 14 March to command an army and a fleet for the 'keeping of the seas', initially intended for defence of Calais and the English coast but subsequently sent to Aquitaine, and perhaps this served as a deterrent. It is also possible that differences between Charles VII and Charles the Bold, Duke of Burgundy, within whose lands Calais lay, prevented the King going ahead with his plans. Whatever the reasons, Calais remained in English hands.[21]

---

20 Chartier, *Chronique de Charles VII, Roi de* France, vol.2, pp.313–23. Leseur, *Histoire de Gaston IV,* vol.1, pp.208–217.
21 Fresne de Beaucourt, *Histoire de Charles VII,* vol.5, pp.53–56. Susan Rose, *Calais, An English Town in France, 1347–1558* (Woodbridge: The Boydell Press, 2008), pp.76–7. A. J. Pollard, *John Talbot and the War in France, 1427–1453* (Barnsley: Pen & Sword, 2005), pp.134–5.

7

John Talbot, First Earl of Shrewsbury

John Talbot was the central figure of the English attempt to reverse the situation in Gascony after the surrender of Bordeaux in June 1351. He was almost the only English commander in the later stages of the Hundred Years' War to emerge with any credit, and his heroic death at Castillon made him celebrated in both England and France to such an extent that Castillon has become almost synonymous with him. Before looking at the final stages of the French conquest of Gascony and the Battle of Castillon, it may be worthwhile to try to gauge what type of man he was and to examine his military career before he arrived in Gascony in October 1452.

John Talbot was born into a family of Anglo-Norman ancestry. He was probably born in 1387, the second son of Richard Talbot, fourth Lord Talbot. John Talbot's father died when John was still a boy and his widowed mother married Thomas Nevill. Under the terms of the marriage, John married Thomas Nevill's heiress, his daughter Maud. When Nevill died in 1407, Talbot inherited his stepfather's title and lands as Lord Furnival of Sheffield. In 1418, his elder brother, Gilbert, died and four years later Gilbert's sole daughter and heiress died in childhood. In the same year, Talbot succeeded to the barony of Talbot and was created earl of Shrewsbury. This sequence of events made John Talbot, 1st Earl of Shrewsbury, one of the richest peers of England.

As was the case with many young noblemen in the Middle Ages, his military career started young, and he was in positions of command while still a teenager. It is possible that he fought at the Battle of Shrewsbury in 1403 when he was 16 years of age; the same age that Edward the Black Prince had been when he participated in the Battle of Crécy in 1346. In December 1404, then around 17 or 18 years old, he took command, as Lord Furnival's deputy, of the garrisons of two castles on the border between Shropshire and Wales. He was subsequently closely involved in the protracted repression of Owain Glyn Dŵr's revolt, which had flared up in 1400, until its end in 1409. In 1414, still only 27, he was sent to Ireland as Henry V's lieutenant. His objective was to protect the lands held by the English from the frequent attacks of Irish rebels, and he was highly successful in restoring stability. His experience in Ireland and Wales was formative. This was not the sort of warfare where there would be set-piece battles – his successes relied on raids to wear down the Welsh and then the Irish, through speed, surprise, and terror. He left Ireland in 1419, but by then had built a reputation as a formidable and fearsome fighter and commander; a reputation that was to remain with him for the rest of his life.

In 1420 Talbot went to serve in France for the first time. He participated in the siege of Melun but returned to England to participate in the celebrations for the coronation of Henry V's new wife Catherine de Valois. He was back in France by mid–1421 and was present at the siege of Meaux from November 1421 until May 1422, when he returned to England once again to sort out his personal affairs after the inheritance of the Lordship of Talbot and the death of his wife Maud.

Among Talbot's traits were a strong combative nature and a violent temper, which he displayed not only on the battlefield but also in civil life. He was a constant thorn in the side of the King and his councillors. A quarrel with the Earl of Arundel in 1413 led to his imprisonment in the Tower of London by Henry V. It is possible that his appointment to Ireland the following year was in part to get him out of the way. In 1423, back in England from France, he was involved in a private war in Herefordshire. The argument was taken to Parliament, and in the same session Talbot made accusations against the Earl of Ormond. Feuding with the Lady of Abergavenny followed, and in one brawl in late 1425 or early 1426, one of his brothers was killed. A further dispute followed, this time with Lord Grey of Ruthen concerning parliamentary precedence. There must have been much relief when in 1427 the Duke of Bedford, Regent of France since the death of Henry V in 1422, decided to take Talbot with him to France.

Talbot's experience in Wales and Ireland was to serve him well in his first appointment as a commander in France. His first action was to go to the support of the Earl of Warwick to recapture Pontorson, five miles south of Mont-Saint-Michel in Normandy, from the Bretons. Talbot was then part of the besieging force at Montargis, east of Orléans and 60 miles south of Paris, that was driven off by the French on 5 September 1427. The same day Sir John Fastolf was surprised in a minor skirmish in Maine, and a number of places rose in revolt encouraged by this success. Bedford then appointed Talbot as his lieutenant and as governor of the Counties of Maine and Anjou with the objective of completing the conquest of Maine and suppressing the revolt in those areas already conquered. Talbot spent the winter preparing for the forthcoming operations. In the spring he launched a savage campaign destroying castles and burning towns, recovering a number of lost places, and extending the conquest to the west of Maine. In May the inhabitants of Le Mans opened the gates to a French army and the English garrison withdrew to the castle. Talbot quickly came to the relief of the castle, took the French by surprise and drove them off. He showed no mercy for the townsmen who had opened the gates to the French, and those who had collaborated in the treachery were hanged. With the departure of

THE BATTLE OF CASTILLON 1453

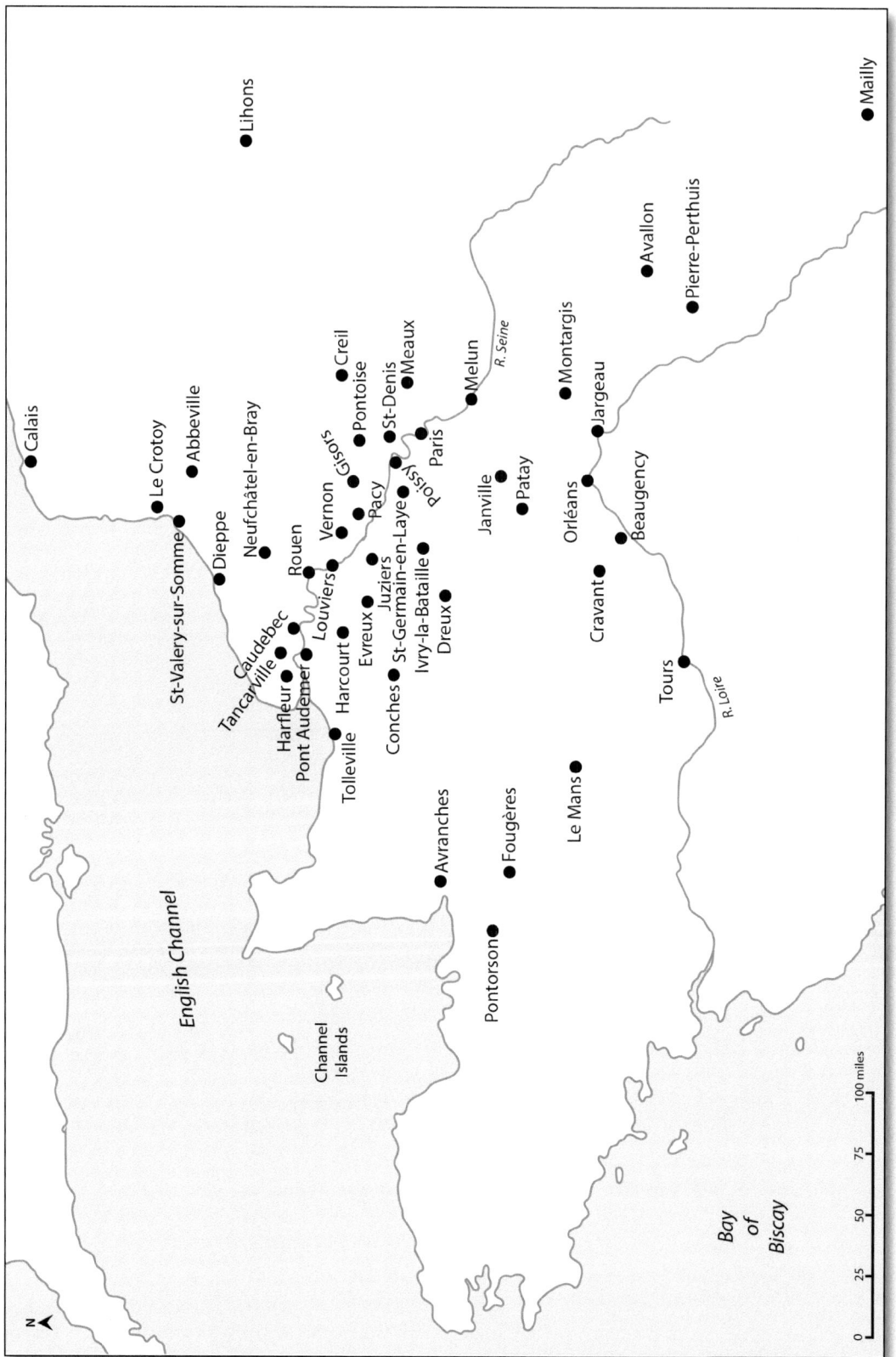

Talbot in Normandy and Northern France, 1427–49

the French from Le Mans, the remaining places, which had rebelled, were retaken without opposition and by June 1428 Talbot had restored complete control over the county. His success, and the manner of its achievement, made him notorious with the French and cemented his reputation as an effective commander.

In the summer of 1428, Bedford began a campaign to take Orléans. Talbot was present in the early stages, including the capture of Beaugency, Meung and Jargeau, but not it seems at the opening of the siege of Orléans itself. However, he was certainly present at the end when the English abandoned the siege and withdrew. The English army was then divided to defend the bridgeheads on the Loire at Beaugency, Meung and Jargeau. Jargeau fell to the French, and they then turned their attention to Beaugency and Meung, held respectively by Talbot and Lord Scales. The French took the bridge at Meung and pressed onto Beaugency. Talbot and Scales hurriedly moved north with a small force to join Sir John Fastolf who had arrived at Janville-en-Beauce, some 30 miles from Beaugency. There was apparently an intense argument between the cautious Fastolf and the aggressive Talbot. Fastolf thought it more prudent to withdraw while Talbot was all for taking the offensive to relieve Beaugency.

Talbot prevailed and the English moved towards Beaugency only to find themselves faced by a superior French army waiting for them and drawn up for battle. Talbot acknowledged that the bridgeheads could not be saved and agreed to a withdrawal as the best option. It was too late; at midday on 18 June the French fell upon the English army resting near Patay, 20 miles north of Beaugency. Talbot and Scales, with the rear-guard, were overwhelmed before they could organise their defence. Both were captured and Talbot was wounded. However, Fastolf, with the vanguard, was able to fight his way out to safety. Talbot was held as a prisoner until the spring of 1433, when he was released in exchange for the senior French commander Poton de Xaintrailles who had been captured in 1431. Talbot briefly returned to England, but by mid-July 1433 had agreed to go back to France.

During his captivity the course of the war had changed significantly. The English were now on the defensive. No longer was the objective to expand their possessions, now they had to defend Paris and repel French incursions into Normandy. The alliance with the Duke of Burgundy was key to England holding on in France, and Talbot was despatched to support the Burgundians in the capture of Pacy-sur-Eure, Avallon, Cravant, Mailly and Pierrre-Perthuis. After this campaign he returned to England once again but by the spring of 1434 Talbot was back in France, initially as captain of Neufchâtel-en-Bray and Gisors and lieutenant-general of the Île-de-France. In June he was appointed as lieutenant-general for all the land between the rivers Seine, Oise and the Somme and the sea. He thus had the responsibility for all the eastern part of English held territory, while the Earl of Arundel commanded the forces in the west. Talbot spent the summer consolidating the hold on the territory and relieving the pressure on Paris. For his success he was rewarded by Bedford with the title of Count of Clermont.

Talbot's objective for 1435 appears to have been to further consolidate his hold on Paris, but he was called back to England in the summer to raise more troops. While he was away Arundel was defeated and killed at Gerberoy. Saint-Denis, only five miles north of Paris, fell to the French, and from there they were able to launch raids on Paris at will. Talbot was back in France with his reinforcements towards the end of July to tackle the problem. However, the pressure of operations elsewhere meant that Saint-Denis was not retaken until the beginning of October. Meanwhile, in September two disasters had befallen the English cause. First, the Duke of Bedford died on 14 September and secondly, on 21 September, Charles VII and the Duke of Burgundy had agreed the Treaty of Arras. The English in a matter of a week had lost a capable and respected leader and the ally who had been critical to their success. With the benefit of hindsight, the loss of Burgundy as an ally could only have one outcome: the eventual loss of English France.

During the latter months of 1435 and early 1436 Talbot was fully occupied with events in Normandy. A peasant revolt, supported by French troops, had threatened Caudebec and Rouen. The revolt was crushed with great brutality by Talbot and the situation restored by the end of January 1436, but now the priority was the defence of Paris. The situation was becoming critical: Saint-Germain-en-Laye, 12 miles west of the capital and blocking access to Paris along the Seine from Normandy, had fallen to the French in December 1435, and Pontoise, 16 miles north-west of Paris and controlling access by road from the north, had fallen in February 1436. Reinforcements were sent to Paris at around the same time as Pontoise fell.

The siege of Paris began in early March, and an attempt in early April to send supplies into the city was unable to break through the French siege lines. On 13 April 1436 the city fell, and four days later the garrison, which had retreated into the bastille, surrendered and marched out to return to Rouen.

French operations continued in Normandy and threatened Rouen and the whole English position in eastern Normandy, but 5,000 men arrived with the Duke of York and, fortunately for the English commanders, the French activities were poorly coordinated, and the crisis passed. However, the focus of English policy now shifted. The claim to the Kingdom of France had become wholly unrealistic and the best that could be hoped for was to hold on to Normandy.

At the risk of oversimplification of a highly complex situation, the next eight years, until the Treaty of Tours brought an uneasy peace, was marked by a transition of the Duchy of Normandy from being an essentially French administered English province to a province under English occupation. Whereas until the early 1430s the defence of Normandy had been borne almost entirely by the duchy, as the years went by the burden on England steadily increased. A burden that the English Parliament was increasingly reluctant to accept. Perhaps it was never admitted as such, but the English seemed prepared to abandon the claim to the Crown of France in return for total sovereignty over Normandy. Substantial forces were maintained, largely in 38 garrisons, with small field armies, which could be supplemented in times of need with men drawn from the garrisons. In addition, in most years reinforcements were sent from England for a six-month period over the summer. Throughout this time the governorship and the senior military appointments changed frequently. It was fortunate for the English that throughout these years the French remained divided and ill-organised, and the results of Jacques Coeur's reforms in financing the war effort had not yet been fully felt. Talbot's position in the defence of Normandy remained central. Although his appointments changed several times, including the prestigious appointment of Marshal of France for much of the time. One thing remained constant up to the Treaty of Tours – Talbot's responsibility for the defence of eastern Normandy, which bore the brunt of the fighting.

The English objectives after the dangers of 1435–36 were clear: to recover and hold the eastern borders of Normandy, to hold as many outposts as possible in the Île de France, and to recover control of the Pays de Caux (broadly the area of western Normandy from the Seine estuary along the coast to Dieppe and to the south Caudebec). The first two objectives were largely Talbot's responsibility, although he was also employed in the Pays de Caux on occasion. Operations by both armies during the years up to the Treaty of Tours were to be hampered by the devastation throughout Normandy. It was impossible for either side to find sufficient provisions to maintain large armies in the field and fighting centred around the capture and defence of towns and fortresses.

In late January 1437, Talbot, with an army reinforced by men from the Duke of York's forces in western Normandy, took Ivry (now Ivry-la-Bataille) on the Eure and then turned north-east to march 25 miles to take Pontoise – key to the control of the Seine between Rouen and Paris – which had been lost almost exactly a year before. The operation was carried out in typical Talbot fashion: a siege of such a strong town during the winter was out of the question, and he opted for a surprise assault. He capitalised on the river being frozen and the garrison celebrating Mardi Gras. An advanced party entered the gates disguised as peasants on the way to market and the main body scaled the walls having crossed the frozen river. The surprise was complete, and the French commanders fled.

Talbot attempted to repeat the feat with Paris on 16–17 February. However, the French were on their guard, and he withdrew. With Pontoise secured Talbot mopped up numerous towns and fortresses. From the summer he was engaged in the Pays de Caux, notably in the prolonged, but ultimately successful, siege of Tancarville, on the right bank of the Seine near the estuary, and a vital objective before Harfleur could be retaken. Tancarville fell in mid-November, and Talbot moved to the east with the objective of relieving the siege of Le Crotoy, a port town on the Bay of the Somme.

Once again speed and boldness were in evidence. He crossed at the ford of Blanchetaque, famously used by Edward III before the Battle of Crécy in 1346, under the eyes of the besiegers. Rather than tackling the besieging force head on he led a rapid raid of destruction and terror in Picardy.

Despite the presence of the Duke of Burgundy close by at Abbeville, he went unmolested. His tactics worked and with the threat of Talbot in their rear, the besieging force withdrew. Operations continued during the rest of 1437 and early 1438 with the capture of several small fortresses and escorted resupply operations to English outposts.

In the summer of 1438 Talbot was back in the Pays de Caux, participating in an unsuccessful siege of Harfleur. In December he recaptured, with a mixture of his hallmark of surprise helped by treachery within the garrison, the important town of Saint-Germain-en-Laye. At the end of the year, the English could reflect on three successful years: other than Harfleur and Dieppe, and their immediate surroundings, the Pays de Caux had been retaken, and eastern Normandy had been secured. On the debit side only one important place had been lost – Montargis in December 1437. Talbot had stamped his mark on the campaigns.

Much of 1439 was relatively quiet as the English attempted to negotiate a peace settlement with the French. Exceptions were the fall of Meaux, where Talbot arrived too late to relieve the garrison before the date set for its surrender on 15 September 1439. The French then targeted Avranches in western Normandy. Talbot was one of the commanders of the army sent to relieve the town and this time he was successful: the English fell upon the besieging force by surprise at night and routed it.

In early 1440, Talbot served under the Earl of Somerset with an army raiding deep into Picardy. The objective was to persuade the Duke of Burgundy to sign a separate peace with England. A great deal of plunder was taken and Folleville and Lihons were captured, in the latter case with Talbot's legendary brutality with a church containing those inhabitants who had taken refuge within being set alight. Talbot's next operation was in the siege of Harfleur between July and late October, when the garrison surrendered after a relief force that had attacked Talbot's section of the siege works was driven off. While the English had been engaged at Harfleur the French had taken Conches-en-Ouche and Louviers, creating a dangerous salient which threatened the Seine between Rouen and Pontoise. In the winter of 1440–1441 the English commanders joined forces with the objective of retaking the lost ground, but Talbot was plagued with problems in recruiting and retaining men. Things dragged on without sufficient men being mustered to retake the lost towns. Nevertheless, in May Talbot set off to recover Dieppe. Meanwhile, Charles VII had laid siege to Creil on the Oise. Talbot started to gather supplies for relief of Creil, but he could not be everywhere at once. He was too late, and the town surrendered on 24 May 1441.

Talbot kept the relief column together, however, since the French were now advancing to threaten Pontoise, the French opened their siege on 6 June. A few days later Talbot set up his headquarters at Vernon, about 27 miles west of the town. On 22 June, he succeeded in entering Pontoise with Lord Scales, who was to remain to take charge of the defence, and reinforcements and supplies. Talbot brought in further supplies towards the end of the month. In July, the Duke of York arrived with a strong force of fresh troops, and Talbot and York joined forces at Juziers, 11 miles west of Pontoise. They entered Pontoise unopposed on 16 July 1441 and resupplied the town. A rare opportunity seemed to be available to face the French army in battle, but the French were cautious and withdrew.

It is not entirely clear what happened over the next few days, but it seems that towards the end of July Talbot made a daring and only narrowly unsuccessful attempt to seize Charles VII at Poissy. Apparently angered by his failure he sacked the town. Over the next two months Talbot continued to resupply Pontoise and Charles VII renewed the siege in mid-August. He was unable to cut off the resupply but eventually in late September opted for an assault following a heavy artillery barrage, and he took the town on 19 September 1441. Although this was a defeat for the English, the long and resolute defence, largely due to Talbot having kept supply lines open, had kept the French at bay and prevented an invasion of Normandy.

A remaining section of the medieval walls of Poissy. (Peter Hoskins)

Elsewhere in Normandy, the French had established a salient from the south as far as the Seine and taken important towns including Évreux. Later in 1441 Talbot was appointed lieutenant-general for the defence of Normandy.

In early 1442, Talbot returned to England for the first time since 1435. He went with councillors from the duchy to plead for more help. He attempted to raise an army of 2,500 men, but England was tired of war, and he faced considerable difficulty in recruiting men. He finally recruited enough men, but with ten archers for every man-at-arms instead of the usual ratio of three to one. Talbot was created Earl of Shrewsbury in May. He returned to France the following month with his newly mustered army. Operations in the following months brought both success and failure. Conches was retaken in September. However, an attempt at the siege of Dieppe, the last remaining French foothold in the Pays de Caux, had to be abandoned. The initial force of around 1,500 men, which arrived in early November, was inadequate for a formal siege. To add to the woes of Shrewsbury (the name we shall now use to reflect John Talbot's elevation to the peerage), some of his men mutinied. They had come to the end of their six-month engagement and refused to serve longer. When the Count of Dunois arrived with 1,000 men to reinforce the garrison, Shrewsbury had no alternative but to break off the siege, leaving 500 men in a bastille constructed on a hill overlooking the port.

Shrewsbury's intention was probably to return to Dieppe with a new army in the spring of 1443, but such an effort would have required the deployment of reinforcements expected from England. In the event, the promised troops were diverted to serve with an independent command under the Duke of Somerset. In June, Shrewsbury went to England, once again to try to secure help. His efforts resulted in little more than an assurance of support for Dieppe. By the time he was back in Normandy in August it was too late either to take Dieppe or to save the isolated force in the bastille. On 14 August, the bastille fell to assault. Somerset's campaign was a disaster, and the war came to a halt with the Treaty of Tours, signed on 28 May 1444.

Dieppe Castle. (Peter Hoskins)

Shrewsbury may have hoped to profit from peace by enjoying his Norman estates, but that was not to be and in March 1445, he was reappointed Lieutenant of Ireland. However, in 1448 he was again back in France in command of Lower Normandy. As such he was heavily involved with events at Fougères the following year, including its resupply after it had been taken by Surienne in March. On 31 July 1449 Shrewsbury drew up his army in a strong defensive position between Beaumont-le-Roger and Harcourt. He hoped to tempt Dunois, leading one of two French armies operating in Normandy, into pitched battle. Dunois would not be drawn, and Shrewsbury would not risk leaving his defensive position to attack the French. He withdrew to Rouen, but in doing so he left Pont-Audemer exposed to attack by the Count of Dunois, and it fell to the French on 12 August. Shrewsbury was involved in the defence of Rouen but became a hostage on 29 October 1449 under the terms of its surrender. He remained as a prisoner until the last of the places that should have surrendered under the terms of the rendition of Rouen had passed into French hands. On 11 July 1450, after the surrender of Falaise, he was released but on the condition that he made a pilgrimage to Rome, and he left Normandy for the last time.[1]

---

1   See Pollard, *John Talbot and the War in France, 1427–1453* for a comprehensive account of John Talbot's career.

8

The French Conquest of Gascony – The Second Campaign

(See Maps 5 and 6, pages 67 and 68)

Shrewsbury completed his pilgrimage to Rome and returned to London on 20 December 1450. Perhaps, now being over 60 years old, he hoped for a quiet retirement. This was not to be. Back in England he was involved in the suppression of the simmering discontent which followed the crushing of Jack Cade's rebellion of 1450, a personal, long-running feud with Lord Berkeley, and the political manoeuvring between the Dukes of Somerset and York.

There were worries in England that Charles VII would, having conquered both Normandy and Gascony, attempt to take Calais – the final English foothold in France. After Shrewsbury's appointment on 14 March 1452 to command a fleet for the protection of Calais and the south coast of England, steps were taken in the spring to muster the men and assemble the shipping for his command. On 20 June, Sir Edward Hull and Gervase Clifton were engaged to serve from 17 July to 21 October 1452. Their commissions were limited in scope and still seem to have been defensive in nature. Shrewsbury's commission was renewed on 17 June for a similar period as Clifton and Hull. However, the mission was now broader and suggestive of a more aggressive purpose: '…for the keeping of the sea in which journey he must perform great good.' It is possible that a return to Normandy with an army of 5,000 men was envisaged, and certainly the French took such a threat seriously. However, there had been lobbying in England by prominent Gascons for an expedition to Bordeaux.

When Bordeaux had surrendered, Charles VII had, under the terms of the treaty of 12 June 1451, guaranteed that the Gascons would continue with the privileges they had had under the English. Notably they would be exempt from all taxes raised in the rest of France, and also they would not be required to raise taxes for war without their consent. Much to the discontent of the Gascons, however, the new administration started to raise taxes to pay for the garrisons left in the duchy, arguing that this was for their own good to defend them from any return of the English. A deputation from Bordeaux and Gascony travelled to Bourges in July 1452 to plead their case with Charles VII, for the treaty to be respected. The King was intransigent.

With discontent growing the Earl of Kendal, Jean de Foix-Grailly, and the Lord of Lesparre, Pierre de Montferrant, together with other representatives of Gascon dissidents, made representations to Henry VI. They prevailed upon King Henry VI's advisers to send an army to Gascony, and Shrewsbury was seen as the obvious commander, despite his advancing years. He is said to have been reluctant to take on the command, since when released without ransom by Charles VII he had vowed never to take up arms again against Charles; a vow which he had renewed when in Rome. We shall see later how he managed to reconcile his sense of duty to the King with his sense of honour and chivalry in accepting the appointment.[1] On 1 September, Shrewsbury was appointed at Westminster as Lieutenant of the Duchy of Aquitaine and the following day his powers were set out in detail.[2]

It took some six weeks to raise Shrewsbury's army, which seems to have been around 4,000 strong rather than the 5,000 originally planned. The army was reported to be well equipped in anticipation of a long and mobile campaign. It sailed from England on 17 October, and with favourable winds made the passage in four days to arrive near the estuary of the Gironde on 21 October. They landed near Soulac-sur-Mer on the Atlantic coast in the Médoc.

The arrival of the English army took the French completely by surprise, with the expected destination of the expeditionary force having been Normandy. It seems that initially there was some opposition to the landings from the local population, although it has been suggested that that had more to do with surprise at the landing and mistrust of the initially unidentified invaders than resistance to a return of the English. However, the Lord of Lesparre, whose lands were also in the Médoc, was able to put the minds of the local population at rest and whatever resistance there was, was short-lived and of no significance.

Shrewsbury advanced rapidly, covering 50 miles to arrive close to Bordeaux during the evening of 22 October. The dissidents within Bordeaux prudently kept their heads down until the English approached the town and then opened the gates to Shrewsbury's men the following morning. The commander of the garrison, Olivier de Coëtivy, was blissfully unaware of the danger he faced. When the situation became clear it was evident that his small force of 70 men could not hope to resist and the French fled as best they could, pursued by the English and inhabitants in search of prisoners

---

1 Pollard, *John Talbot and the War in France, 1427–1453*, pp.131–5. Basin, *Histoire de Charles VII et Louis XI*, pp.270 & 275–279. Ribadieu, *Histoire de la Conquête de la Guyenne par les Français,* pp.266–271.
2 Gascon Rolls, gasconrolls.org, C61/139, Membranes 7-17 and 7-27.

to ransom. De Coëtivy went into hiding but was betrayed by an inhabitant greedy for a share of his ransom; he was sent to England by Shrewsbury.

The powers that had been granted to Shrewsbury were extensive, considerably more than those granted to solely a military commander: he was in effect Viceroy and was known to the Gascons as 'King Shrewsbury'. Many towns that had been garrisoned by the French rapidly came back into the English fold. By Christmas the towns of Blanquefort, Libourne, Gensac, Chalais, Montravel, Castillon, Cadillac, Rions, Saint-Macaire, Saint-Émilion, and Langon had all been re-occupied. The towns of La Réole and as far away as Condom (125 miles south-east of Bordeaux), which had not been garrisoned, also returned to the English fold. However, Charles VII had quickly sent reinforcements to Fronsac and Blaye and the towns remained in French hands, as did the important fortress of Bourg, which had a strong garrison, controlling with Blaye the Gironde downstream of Bordeaux. Shrewsbury had rapidly restored control over much of Aquitaine. Charles VII was not drawn into a hasty response. Other than reinforcing Fronsac and Blaye, he decided to bide his time and prepare for the new campaigning season in the spring of 1453. The question was whether Shrewsbury would be able to hold on when the French brought their strength to bear.[3]

The castle at La Réole, a key town on the Garonne river. (Peter Hoskins)

The news of Shrewsbury's success was welcome in London after the setbacks of recent years. An army, commanded by Shrewsbury's son Viscount Lisle, was raised to reinforce the troops already in Gascony. The army, 2,325 strong, was mustered at Dartmouth and Plymouth on 5 March 1453. It arrived in Bordeaux later that month, and with its men Shrewsbury probably had around 7,000 English soldiers at his disposal as a field army for the forthcoming campaign. A fleet of 84 ships had been gathered for the expedition, and with the troops

---

3 Ribadieu, *Histoire de la Conquête de la Guyenne par les Français*, pp.271–283.

came plentiful supplies of salted pork and flour to resupply Bordeaux and provide a reserve in case of siege.[4]

Over the winter, Charles VII had been methodically preparing his response to Shrewsbury's campaign. Troops who had been deployed on the borders with Savoy were recalled, and Jean Bureau spent the early months of the year in manufacturing cannonballs, powder, guns of various calibres suitable for sieges or a set-piece battle, and wagons for transporting powder and balls. While Bureau was busy preparing the artillery, Charles VII was mustering his troops with orders sent out to mobilise men-at-arms, archers, and *franc-archers*. In the spring Charles VII assembled his armies with the objective, similar to his strategy in Normandy, of advancing on several fronts. By May four armies had been assembled, perhaps with as many as 30,000 men. One army, under the Marshals Lohéac and Culant, had the task of advancing down the Dordogne, the second, commanded by the Count of Clermont, was to operate in the Médoc and Entre-Deux-Mers, a third, under the Count of Foix was to move north from Béarne, while the King held the fourth in reserve on the Charente, near Angoulême.

Having received his reinforcements Shrewsbury did not waste time and was first in the field, opening the siege of Fronsac in the spring. The siege seems to have been brief with the garrison commander, Joachim Rouhault, entering into a surrender agreement allowing him to withdraw with his men and their possessions. With this important town back in his hands Shrewsbury returned to Bordeaux. The obvious next objectives would have been Bourg and Blaye to secure English use of the Gironde from the sea upstream to Bordeaux. However, Shrewsbury elected not to try to retake these towns. Perhaps he did not believe that he had the necessary strength to take these places, or perhaps, aware of the gathering French armies, he decided that it was more prudent to keep his army in readiness.

King Charles VII had spent the winter at Tours, and at some point in the spring, he had moved south to Lusignan, 15 miles south-west of Poitiers. At the beginning of June, the French offensive began in earnest and the King moved further south to Saint-Jean-d'Angely, 80 miles north of Bordeaux. Chalais, 30 miles north of the Dordogne, seems to be one of the rare, if not the only, place held in this area by the Anglo-Gascons to have shown any resistance. Joachim Rouhault, who had returned to join Charles VII after the surrender of Fronsac, and other commanders from the army commanded by Lohéac and Culant, arrived outside the town around 5 June. Rouhault and his companions had a substantial force of some 400 to 500 lances and an unknown number of archers. The Anglo-Gascon garrison was 160 strong. On the fifth day of the siege the French succeeded in entering the town through a breach that had been made in the walls. Half of the garrison had lost their lives during the assault, the remainder had withdrawn to a tower and continued to resist for a further three days until the last of the

---

4 Pollard, *John Talbot and the War in France, 1427–1453*, pp.131–135. Ribadieu, *Histoire de la Conquête de la Guyenne par les Français*, p.283.

THE BATTLE OF CASTILLON 1453

garrison surrendered. Under the customs of the period, the garrison of a town or fortress that surrendered could expect their lives to be spared. The French commanders were prepared to recognise the valour of the English defenders and released them under ransom. The Gascons, however, were considered as traitors having rebelled after the terms of the surrender in 1451, and they were executed by decapitation. An Anglo-Gascon force is reported to have been sent to relieve Chalais, but if so it arrived too late and on hearing of the fate of the garrison hastened back to Bordeaux.[5]

In early June, Saint-Sever, 75 miles south of Bordeaux, fell to the Count of Foix, perhaps now operating with the Count of Clermont, who was moving through Bazas and north towards Bordeaux and the Médoc. On 21 June, Shrewsbury sent heralds with a letter to Clermont, now in the Médoc to the west of Bordeaux. He proposed battle, ostensibly to save the countryside and peasantry from unnecessary damage and suffering, but the underlying reason was probably that he was hoping to eliminate one of the armies that threatened his hold on Gascony before the forces opposing him could combine. Shrewsbury said that he would be in position in three days in an open space suitable for battle and asked Clermont to remain in the area until he was ready. Clermont replied that he would wait for the three days proposed and join him in battle.

Shrewsbury advanced to the village of Martignas-sur-Jalle (ten miles west of Bordeaux and close to the present airport). He is said to have had between 6,000 and 7,000 men with him. However, it seems that he was initially unaware that the Count of Foix had joined forces with Clermont. When the news reached him that he faced the combined forces of Clermont and Foix any hope of eliminating one army had gone, and the balance of forces was now much less favourable. Shrewsbury decided that prudence was the better part of valour and, after only two hours at Martignas, withdrew to Bordeaux. When Clermont and Foix arrived, they found the proposed battlefield deserted. The French set off in pursuit of Shrewsbury's army, but, other than a contingent of archers who were attacked and defeated, the Anglo-Gascon army returned safely to Bordeaux. Food and forage were in short supply in the Médoc, and the armies of the Counts of Clermont and Foix separated again to enable them to find sufficient supplies while they waited for the opportunity to meet Shrewsbury in battle if he ventured out.

After the capture of Chalais, the French advanced along the Dordogne valley; numerous places which had fallen to the English the previous autumn, including Gensac, which surrendered on 8 July, and Montravel were quickly retaken. The next town in the Dordogne valley on the route towards Bordeaux was Castillon.

There was discussion among the commanders of the army approaching Castilllon whether they should press on directly to Bordeaux or take the time to besiege Castillon. The two Bureau brothers were with the army and

---

5   Chartier, *Chronique de Charles VII, Roi de* France, vol.2, pp.333–335. Ribadieu, *Histoire de la Conquête de la Guyenne par les Français,* pp.285–288.

THE FRENCH CONQUEST OF GASCONY – THE SECOND CAMPAIGN

Jean impressed upon the commanders the importance of taking the town. He stressed that holding fortresses on the Dordogne would be vital as the army advanced on Bordeaux to ensure resupply: 'Castillon is the key to the Dordogne, which is the route which leads to Bordeaux; there is nothing we could do to our greater profit than take it.'[6]

The siege opened on 12 or 13 July. When the news reached Bordeaux, it is reported that Shrewsbury was reluctant to go to the relief of Castillon, preferring to wait for the French to approach Bordeaux. However, the people of Bordeaux argued that it was implicit in their having opened their gates that he should go to the relief of Castillon. It is said that he reluctantly accepted their urging to relieve Castillon. Other sources suggest that, on the contrary, he saw the opportunity to eliminate what he assessed as a relatively weak army compared with those of the Counts of Clermont and Foix facing him in the Médoc and that it would be sensible to destroy the army on the Dordogne first. This latter seems more probable, but whatever the true reason he set out, and he rested at Libourne overnight on 16 July, 10 miles to the west of Castillon. He was accompanied by his son, Viscount Lisle, and Jean de Foix-Grailly, Viscount of Castillon and Earl of Kendal. Shrewsbury sent out scouts, both to gather intelligence and to announce his arrival to the garrison. The Anglo-Gascon army arrived at Castillon around daybreak the following morning.[7]

---

6 Ribadieu, *Histoire de la Conquête de la Guyenne par les Français*, p.289, n.1.
7 Ribadieu, *Histoire de la Conquête de la Guyenne par les Français*, pp.286–289. Fresne de Beaucourt, *Histoire de Charles VII*, vol.5, pp.268–272.

9

The Battle of Castillon, 17 July 1453

The Sources and Uncertainties

There are 11 surviving texts written by contemporaries of the battle, all are French. None are written by participants, in contrast with those from Poitiers and Agincourt, but the writers probably drew on the testimony and evidence of those present at the battle. There are discrepancies between the accounts concerning the date of the battle, the size of the two armies, the numbers of casualties, Shrewsbury's age, and the course of the battle. Nevertheless, the main elements of the battle can be ascertained.

Some sources are vague concerning the date of the battle and others are inconsistent with other elements of their accounts. However, two documents written in the immediate aftermath of the battle do agree. These two sources are an anonymous letter dated 19 July written at Angoulême, and a letter from Charles VII, at Rochefoucauld when news of the battle reached him, to the people of Lyon on 22 July 1453. Both letters state that the battle took place on 17 July. For those who seek precision these dates are in the Julian calendar in use until 1582. The date of the battle in the Gregorian calendar would be 28 July.

As is often the case in accounts of medieval battles, numbers of combatants vary considerably between accounts and are usually in round numbers. For Shrewsbury's Anglo-Gascon army estimates vary from 4,000 to 5,000 to more than 10,000. Only one chronicler attempts to break this down between cavalry and infantry giving a figure of 800 to 1,000 cavalry and between 4,000 and 6,000 infantry. The nearest to contemporary source, the Angoulême letter, reports the army as 7,000 strong. This is conveniently close to the median figure and in the absence of precise evidence is as close as we are likely to get to an accurate figure. English armies at the time usually had a high proportion of archers; one source suggests 800 archers, a relatively low proportion, no doubt brought from England by

THE BATTLE OF CASTILLON, 17 JULY 1453

Shrewsbury in late 1452 and by his son in the spring of 1453. However, his force would also have included Gascons, and the infantry with Shrewsbury would predominantly have been spearmen. Shrewsbury would certainly have been concerned about the risk posed to Bordeaux by the armies of Clermont and Foix still in the Médoc, and can be expected to have left a substantial garrison in the town, almost certainly including some of the archers available to him.

The figures for the French army, commanded by Jacques I de Chabannes and Jean V de Beuil, are equally uncertain. Some sources only talk in terms of lances while others give an overall total. The highest figure quoted is 10,000, but this is an eighteenth-century English account. The contemporary French sources that address the total fall between 6,000 and 8,000 men. Therefore, we probably have two armies of roughly the same strength.

Some chroniclers give Shrewsbury's age as eighty, while others refer to him as being old and worn out. He is usually thought to have been born in 1387, give or take a year or so, and so he was probably in his mid to late sixties – old for battle by any standards and in any period, and certainly so in the fifteenth century.

The Porte de Fer, constructed in the thirteenth century, is the only surviving element of the medieval fortifications of Castillon. This view was taken looking out from the town towards the Dordogne. (Peter Hoskins)

The Battlefield

Before it received its modern name of Castillon-la-Bataille the town was known as Castillon-sur-Dordogne, from its position on the river, or Castillon-en-Perigord. The Dordogne is a significant river, almost 200 yards wide; the town stands on the right bank, to the north, and in the Middle Ages had a castle, which was demolished in the seventeenth century, at the eastern end. A flood plain extends to the east of the town on the right bank, bounded on the north by the river Lidoire, and behind which is high ground. This river is much less important that the Dordogne but was sufficiently wide and deep to be a significant obstacle for mounted troops and infantry. With the Lidoire as a natural obstacle at the back 700 labourers had, over about four days, constructed an encampment a little over a mile to the east of the town in preparation for the siege. With the work having started at the beginning of the siege on 13 July, it must have

THE BATTLE OF CASTILLON 1453

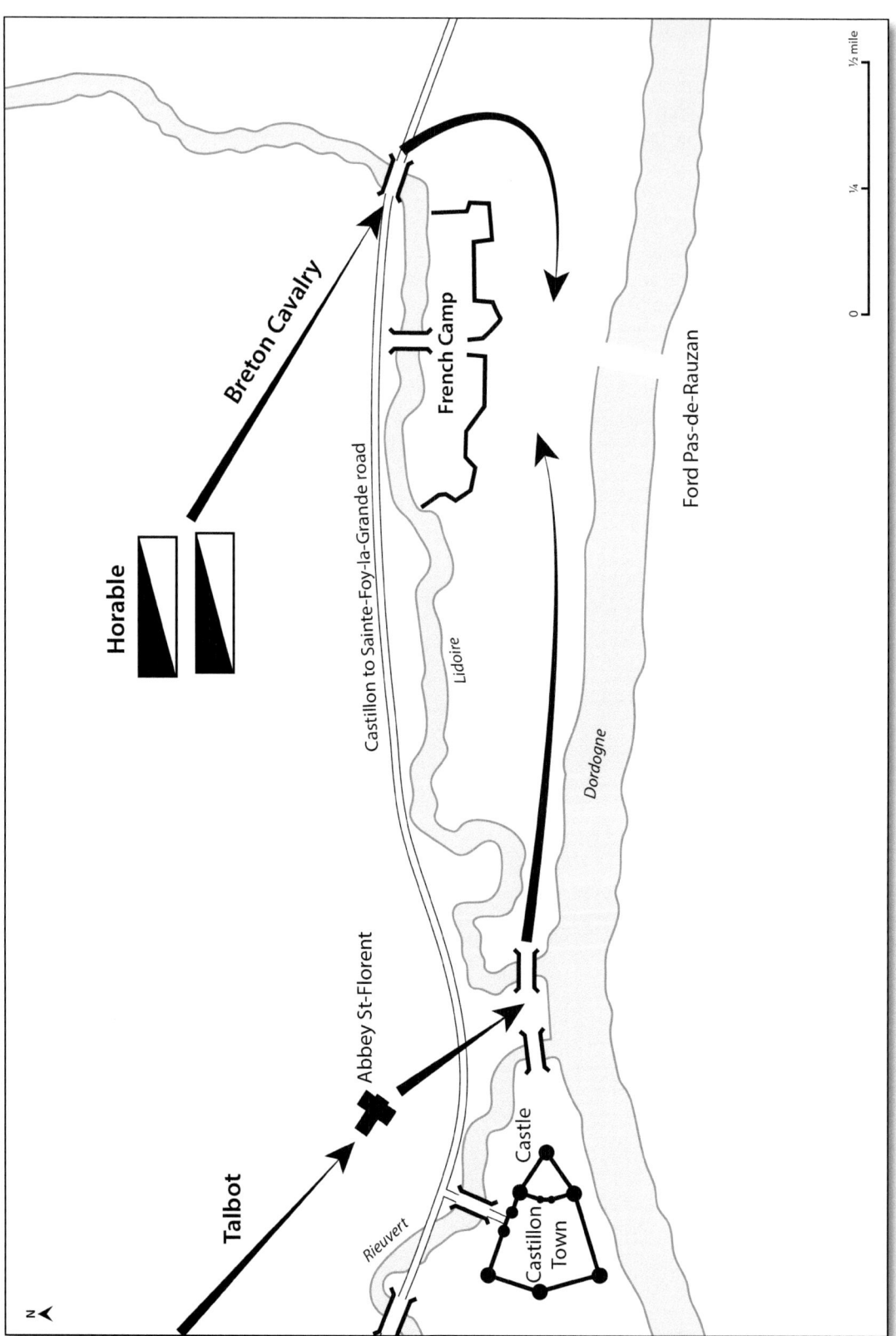

Castillon – the Battlefield, 17 July 1453

been completed very shortly before the battle. The distance from the town, and its orientation from west to east, indicates that it was intended as a protected depot or artillery park for the 300 assorted cannon of the army (said to comprise bombards, veuglaires, culverins, serpentines and ribaudequins) and the associated transport, horses, and ammunition, plus the army's baggage. Thus, the defended camp was not a siege work as such, but as was common at the time when a protracted siege was expected and in keeping with Jean Bureau's concept of operations, a means of defence for the besiegers in case of attempted relief – certainly a risk in this case. The park was a little over half-a-mile long and at its widest, 250 yards deep. It was defended by ditches and palisades on embankments formed by the earth dug from the ditches and it followed a meandering path south of the river. It has been suggested that the ditches were filled with water from the Lidoire. The reason for the line that the defences follow is a matter for speculation. The various salients and re-entrants suggest a deliberate design to enable enfilading fire. However, the pattern was very irregular, and it may be that the line of the defences followed the former bed of the Lidoire. This would have been a practical way of minimising the work, but if so the apparent salients and re-entrants were entirely fortuitous. About halfway along the southern side of the park, there was a deep re-entrant which is thought to have served as an entrance at its open end, possibly with a bridge over the ditch at the closed end. Behind the re-entrant there was a ford across the Lidoire, which could have served as a secondary entrance. A further feature of the battlefield is a stream called the Rieuvert. The Lidoire and Rieuvert now flow separately into the Dordogne, but until the late seventeenth century the river and the stream shared a common confluence with the Dordogne, and there was probably a bridge over the Rieuvert and Lidoire close to the Dordogne. The opening phase of the battle took place at

The line of the ditches and palisade of the French camp are still visible after more than five centuries. (Peter Hoskins)

the Abbey of Saint-Florent, about a quarter of a mile north of the town. The abbey has long since gone, but it is thought to have been roughly on the site of the present railway station.[1] About half-a-mile north of the battlefield was a hill, at the time known as Orable and now as Horable, which overlooked the encampment.

View from the battlefield north to the Horable from where the Breton cavalry made their decisive attack to rout the Anglo-Gascon army. (Peter Hoskins)

The Battle

Charles VII, in his letter written five days after the battle, recounts that the fighting started at around nine o'clock in the morning and lasted something more than an hour. Other accounts say that Shrewsbury arrived at first light having ridden through the night from Libourne, with his infantry following on behind. The two times are not necessarily inconsistent. According to some sources, the first contact was between Anglo-Gascon mounted men, and 800 *franc-archers* stationed at the abbey. The archers were quickly driven off and pursued, with between 100 and 120 killed by mounted Anglo-Gascons. An alternative account is that news of the arrival

---

[1] 'Schemas des Modifications du Lit de la Lidoire (1703)'. 'Plan du Camp Français (L. Drouyn 1865)'. 'L'Assaut du Camp Retranché', *Les plus Anciens Recits de la Bataille de Castillon*, Le Groupe de Recherches Historiques et de Sauvetages Archéologiques du Castillonnais, undated and without page numbers. A. H. Burne, 'The French Camp at Castillon', *The Royal Engineers Journal*, vol. LXII (December 1948), pp.290-1. 'Le Prieuré Saint-Florent et son annexe Notre–Dame de Colles, paroisse de Castillon, juridictionde Montravel', http://jm33500.canalblog.com/archives/2006/01/17/4454676.html.

of Shrewsbury's army spread quickly, and the men at the abbey, along with other French troops outside the town, began retiring to the encampment before the arrival of Shrewsbury. The Anglo-Gascons pursued the archers and the retiring troops. This version agrees with the other in that the cavalry overran the archers, who were on foot, and some 100 to 120 were reported as having been killed. Incidentally, this is the only figure that we have for French losses concerning the battle.

There was now a pause in battle, which could account for the difference between first light and nine o'clock, and the Anglo-Gascons who had pursued the fleeing archers halted on the flood plain. At this point Shrewsbury appears to have intended to await the assembly of all of his army before attacking the French. During the pause, stocks of French provisions and wine at the abbey were distributed among the Anglo-Gascon troops. While he waited Shrewsbury, as was common practice at the time before a battle, decided to take mass at the abbey. It is said that during mass word came to him from a member of the garrison that the French were breaking camp and leaving to avoid combat. The assessment that the French were withdrawing seems to have been based on the sight of clouds of dust over the encampment. However, the dust was not caused by the withdrawal of the army but by valets taking horses out of the encampment, presumably out of the rear entrance and through the ford over the Lidoire, to find pasture. It seems that Shrewsbury underestimated the strength of the army which he faced and that, at this point at least, did not appreciate the importance of the defended camp. The choice that he faced was to await the arrival of the last of his infantry and his artillery to concentrate the maximum of force, but thus running the risk of finding that his opponent had fled, or attacking with the men already available with the intent of destroying one of the armies threatening his hold on Gascony.

Shrewsbury took the second option and broke off mass to muster his men. In the meantime, during the pause between the arrival of the Anglo-Gascon army at the abbey and Shrewsbury's decision to attack, the French had taken advantage of the time available to withdraw their men within the encampment and array their guns behind the palisade and the ditch. Thus, whatever the initial intention in constructing the encampment, it was to become a fortress and the focal point for the battle.

The Anglo-Gascon army advanced east across the flood plain, crossing the Lidoire and Rieuvert to approach the encampment. Contemporary accounts say that Shrewsbury was astonished to see the strength of the encampment with its deep ditches, palisades and guns and an army more numerous than he had expected. His standard-bearer, Thomas Everingham, a long-standing member of Shrewsbury's retinue, urged caution. He advised Shrewsbury not to risk everything in a hasty attack. Everingham suggested that the earl should either await the arrival of all his infantry and artillery and then launch his attack, or he should besiege the camp, forcing the French either to surrender or to leave the protection of the camp to confront the Anglo-Gascon army. Everingham is also said to have impressed on the earl that the local population was favourable to his cause and that, unlike in the case of the French, the Anglo-Gascon army would have no problem with supplies. Shrewsbury reproached Everingham for his uncharacteristic timidity and ordered him to carry the standard to the ditch. Although Shrewsbury remained mounted, he ordered the men-at-arms to dismount and fight on foot – a common tactic for English armies throughout the Hundred Years' War. Shrewsbury remained mounted and the reason for this is attributed by several chroniclers to his advancing years, but it may simply have been that he wanted to be able to see the progress of the battle.

The assault was launched across the width of the encampment, although there seems to have been a concentration around the entrance. The charging troops cried 'Talbot! Saint George!', carrying the standards of Saint George and of the Trinity into battle to join that of Shrewsbury planted at the ditch by Everingham to signal the start of the battle. One chronicler also relates that the Anglo-Gascons carried several standards bearing insulting and malicious references to the French loyal to Charles VII. The French inflicted heavy losses from the outset with artillery fire, crossbows, and javelins. Nevertheless, the attack was pressed home, and the Anglo-Gascons crossed the ditch to reach the palisade, and fierce hand-to-hand fighting ensued. Both sides were tiring, but the Anglo-Gascon infantry was now arriving, thus bringing fresh men into the battle. In addition, the English artillery was now approaching Castillon.

On the high ground at Horable, there were some 300 Breton lances, 1,800 men, commanded by Gilles de Tournemine, Lord of Hunaudaye, and Jean III, Lord of Montauban. It was at this critical point when the day was in the balance that the Bretons were ordered to join the battle. Since the subsequent flight of the Anglo-Gascons was to the west it can be safely assumed that the cavalry headed south-east and crossed the Lidoire, either by a bridge or a ford, roughly where the current D936 crosses the river. They then swung right to strike the Anglo-Gascon army in its right flank. The blow coming at a critical point in the battle was reminiscent of a similar manoeuvre at the Battle of Poitiers almost 100 years before. On that occasion, when the battle looked as though it was starting to go in favour of the French, the then Captal de Buch, Jean de Grailly III, was sent by the Black Prince with mounted men-at-arms and archers in a sweeping manoeuvre out of sight of the French to attack the army of King Jean II in the rear. The result was the collapse of the French attack, the rout of the army and the capture of Jean II. Ironically, on this occasion it was Jean de Foix-Grailly, son of the current Captal de Buch, who was caught by this manoeuvre, where the effect was essentially the same.

The attack on their flank disrupted the Anglo-Gascon attack and allowed the French within and in front of the encampment to surge forward. Jean Bureau also managed to bring his artillery to bear with devastating effect. The result was that the Anglo-Gascon army was routed. During this phase of the battle Shrewsbury's horse was struck and killed by a ball fired from a culverin or serpentine. Shrewsbury was unhorsed and the horse fell upon him. He may also have been wounded by the gun's fire, but, in any case, he was trapped by the body of his horse and finished off by a French archer with a sword or dagger thrust to the throat. One chronicler, Thomas Basin, asserts that the earl, lying wounded, offered a rich ransom in exchange for his life. He goes on to state that the *franc-archers* who found him, in revenge for the killing of archers at the opening of the battle, were not inclined to mercy and rained blows on his body:

> Thus, according to the words of Saint James the Apostle, he was judged without mercy he who had given no mercy to anyone, and according to the word of our Saviour, perished by the sword he who had stuck often with the sword. He had indeed been extremely ferocious and cruel towards the French who, at the end, served him in the same way.[2]

Shrewsbury was unarmed and wearing neither plate nor mail armour, since he had sworn an oath on his release by Charles VII never again to bear arms against the King of France.[3] Shrewsbury's son, Viscount Lisle, was also killed. It is often said that Shrewsbury's standard-bearer, Thomas Everingham, also died in the battle, but as he signed a will in England on 10 November 1453 he must have survived.[4]

The French were concerned to verify that the corpse found on the battlefield was indeed that of John Talbot, Earl of Shrewsbury. Once the battle had finished the Anglo-Gascons had asked for permission to send

The river Dordogne at the point where fleeing Anglo-Gascons attempted to cross the river at the Ford of Rosan. (Peter Hoskins)

---

2 Basin, *Histoire de Charles VII et Louis XI*, pp.285–286 (author's translation).
3 Ribadieu, *Histoire de la Conquête de la Guyenne par les Français*, p.312.
4 http://johnmwatson.blogspot.com/2017/07/everingham-of-rockley-and-stainborough_22.html

heralds to identify their dead. Permission was granted and Shrewsbury's herald confirmed to the French that the body was indeed that of the earl.

The Anglo-Gascon army now fled, no doubt discarding weapons and armour as they went. The French on foot were exhausted and did not pursue the fleeing men, but those who were mounted did. Some of the Anglo-Gascon army fled to the Dordogne, probably trying to cross the river at the Ford of Rosan (near the modern monument to Talbot), and were drowned as they tried to escape, others fled to the safety of the town of Castillon. Between 800 and 2,000 are said to have managed to reach the safety of Castillon. Some fled towards Saint-Émilion, seven miles away, pursued by French cavalry, and some managed to return to Bordeaux. Among those who reached the safety of Castillon were Jean de Foix-Grailly, Earl of Kendal, and the Lords of Monferrant, Rauzan and Anglade. The Lord of Lesparre was with those who fled to Bordeaux, no doubt in fear for his life having been one of the instigators of the English return to Bordeaux and thus breaking his oath to Charles VII.

Some 200 Anglo-Gascon prisoners are reported as being taken after the battle. Casualty figures are unknown for the French, the only mention being of the up to 120 killed at the beginning of the battle. Figures for the English dead vary from 500 to 4,000 or more. Casualties were often considerably higher for a routed army than the victor in the Middle Ages, as fleeing troops, particularly those on foot, were pursued by mounted men. It is likely that men pursued as they sought refuge at Castillon were killed and others drowned in the Dordogne. The French are reported to have buried between 400 and 500 dead from the Anglo-Gascon army. There are also contemporary claims of at least 30 Anglo-Gascons of knightly rank being killed. It was common practice for heralds to check the identity of men of rank killed in battle, and this figure may be reliable. We do not know whether the figure of between 400 and 500 were only the dead on the battlefield or included those who were caught as they fled to Saint-Émilion. If the figure is accurate, we need to add to this those who drowned in the Dordogne. Perhaps, the best that we can say is that the Anglo-Gascon losses probably exceeded 500. On the French side, apart from the archers killed in the opening phase, among notables Jacques de Chabannes is said by some to have died on 20 October 1453 of wounds received at the battle. However, it has also been suggested that he died of either the plague or dysentery caught during the subsequent siege of Bordeaux. Additionally, Jean de Beuil was wounded twice; that both senior French commanders were wounded is perhaps indicative of the ferocity of the fighting.

After the defeat of Shrewsbury's army, the French turned their attention to completing the siege of Castillon and Bureau's guns were brought forward to bombard the walls. The town and castle held out for four days, but the garrison, and survivors from the army within the town, surrendered and were taken prisoner at the mercy of Charles VII. The King reported the number of prisoners taken as 2,000 in a postscript to his letter dated 22 July, in which he recorded the fall of Castillon – this figure would have included both members of the original garrison and those who had fled to the town after the battle. An unknown number escaped the battle to return to Bordeaux. The French had no ships with them and had been unable to complete the siege on the Dordogne side of the town; those who escaped before the fall of the town probably did so by river. Among those captured was Jean de Foix-Grailly, Earl of Kendal, who was sent to Taillebourg and held by Olivier de Coëtivy. Kendal remained a prisoner until January 1460 while the terms of his ransom were negotiated. [5]

Shrewsbury to Blame?

Shrewsbury is often criticised for launching a rash attack. He is accused of replicating the errors of the French at Crécy, Poitiers and Agincourt, attacking a strongly defended position impetuously, and doing so without waiting for the arrival of his infantry and artillery. Is this criticism justified?

As we have seen most of Shrewsbury's long military career was involved with small-scale operations and not major set-piece battles. Indeed, his only major battles were possibly Shrewsbury in 1403, when he was very young and not in a position of command, Patay in 1429 and Castillon. This was by no means unusual for a career soldier of the period: commanders, unless they were unfortunate enough to be surprised, avoided battle unless they considered that the situation was favourable – the consequences of a battle lost were too serious to be taken lightly.

The hallmarks of Shrewsbury's military career were his reputation for moving at speed and for exploiting the element of surprise together with his leadership and his personal courage. However, he was not a rash commander; there were numerous occasions when he refused to be drawn into battle when the odds did not appear to be in his favour: at Beaugency in 1429, at Pontoise in 1441, at Harcourt in 1449, and only a few weeks before Castillon at Martignas when he was faced with the combined armies of the Counts of Clermont and Foix. However, at Patay in 1429 he misjudged the situation and was defeated and captured. The defeat at Castillon was perhaps more a case of misjudgement than rashness.

There are a number of questions concerning his decisions at Castillon about which we can only speculate on answers. Having achieved surprise after having ridden through the night with his mounted troops to arrive

---

5   The account of the battle is drawn from a number of sources: Basin, *Histoire de Charles VII et Louis XI*, pp.282–286. Fresne de Beaucourt, *Histoire de Charles VII*, vol.5, pp.463–464 (Letter from Charles VII, date 22 July 1453). Accounts by Berry Herald *Histoire Chronologique de Roy Charles VII*, by Matthieu de Coucy, and by Enguerran de Monstrelet reproduced in *Les plus Anciens Recits de la Bataille de Castillon*, Le Groupe de Recherches Historiques et de Sauvetages Archéologiques du Castillonnais. Chartier, *Chronique de Charles VII, Roi de France*, vol.3, pp.1–8. Ribadieu, *Histoire de la Conquête de la Guyenne par les Français*, pp.289–316. Leseur, *Histoire de Gaston IV*, vol.2, pp.12–20. Basin, *Histoire de Charles VII et Louis XI*, pp.284–6.

at first light, why did he not press home his advantage? Presumably, at this stage he did not think it likely that the French would withdraw, and he preferred to await the arrival of his infantry and artillery to give him the maximum force with which to engage the enemy. However, we do not know whether his objective was simply to relieve Castillon or to destroy the French army. When he received intelligence, false as it turned out, that the French were withdrawing why did he not conduct reconnaissance to assess the situation before committing to the deployment of his army? If he had appreciated that the French were not withdrawing, and the strength of the French defensive position, he should surely have awaited the remainder of his troops, and particularly the artillery, before joining battle. However, he did not seek to verify the accuracy of the intelligence. When he had arrayed the men that he had available, it became clear that the French were not withdrawing but instead had taken the opportunity during the pause in fighting to withdraw within the artillery park and prepare their defence. Why did he decide to attack at this moment rather than await the arrival of his infantry and artillery? French chroniclers thought that he placed great importance on his reputation and that that would suffice to carry the day. Others suggest that his sense of honour, within his concept of chivalry, would not allow him to withdraw. However, we have already seen that only the month before he had withdrawn in face of the armies of the Counts of Clermont and Foix without any apparent concern for his honour. The question that comes to mind is: why not wait an hour or so? As we have seen his infantry arrived before the end of the battle and the artillery do not seem to have been far behind. The reasons may be more prosaic than honour and personal reputation.

Command and control of medieval armies was notoriously problematic. King Philip VI at Crécy found himself driven by the elan of his vanguard and against his wishes, into battle against a strong defensive position. At Poitiers Jean II lost control of his army at the beginning of the battle. The vanguard of his army launched an uncoordinated and impetuous attack when it appeared that the Black Prince was escaping the army's grasp, and the King had no option but to engage the reminder of his army. At Agincourt, the French were goaded into attacking the English in an uncoordinated fashion by the arrow storm of Henry V's archers.

Having moved close to the French position, and found it to be much stronger than he anticipated, could Shrewsbury really wait? To withdraw temporarily would have been potentially chaotic and exposed his army to attack at a time when they were vulnerable. Additionally, his men were in front of the artillery park and the distance to the Dordogne from the ditches was at its maximum 500 yards. They were well within range of the artillery lining the palisade, and the front ranks would also have been within bow shot. To wait for the remainder of the army would have simply left those already arrayed exposed as easy targets. Again, we have no evidence to that effect, but did the artillery open fire and provoke the attack? It seems probable that they would have opened fire as soon as the English were within range; with the time necessary to reload medieval guns it would be

THE BATTLE OF CASTILLON, 17 JULY 1453

sensible to fire an initial round at maximum range to allow time for the reload before Shrewsbury's men came into contact. There is also another question to which we do not have an answer – was Shrewsbury aware of the Breton troops in reserve on the Horable? If not, then this points further to a lack of reconnaissance.

In conclusion, many aspects of the battle are unclear, and in the absence of a first-hand account from a contemporary English source we may be lacking crucial information which influenced Shrewsbury's decision making. It is difficult with what little we know to escape the judgement that the Anglo-Gascon defeat may have been due to his command decisions and misjudgement. Outcomes in war often turn on fine judgements, and in retrospect Shrewsbury misjudged the strength of his enemy and the capacity of his own army when battle was joined. He may also have underestimated the effectiveness of the French artillery.

The French victory is normally attributed to Jean Bureau's artillery. However, the artillery fire did not prevent the Anglo-Gascons closing to hand-to-hand combat, and the decisive blow was probably the intervention of the Breton cavalry. If Shrewsbury had been true to his reputation for speed and surprise and pressed home his initial attack when he first arrived on the battlefield, he might have caught the bulk of the French army before it could reach the relative safety of the artillery park, and before the artillery could be positioned behind the palisades. With the two armies engaged in hand-to-hand combat the artillery could not have been brought to bear. Maybe it was a closer run battle than is generally thought, and perhaps the role of the artillery was more by accident than design.

The Impact

Within three months of Shrewsbury's defeat the English hold on Gascony had finally collapsed and the Hundred Years' War was over. We can only speculate whether a victory for Shrewsbury at Castillon would have led to a different conclusion. With three other French armies in the field converging on Bordeaux it is difficult to see how he could have defeated the combined strength of the French

The monument to the battle erected in 1888, inscribed:

On this plain, on 17 July 1453, was won the victory which delivered from the English yoke the southern provinces of France and finished the Hundred Years' War. Commander of the French army Jean Bureau, Treasurer of France and Grand Master of Artillery [and] the Count of Penthièvre, commander of the Companies of Ordonnance.

(Peter Hoskins)

THE BATTLE OF CASTILLON 1453

armies. Perhaps an Anglo-Gascon victory at Castillon would simply have delayed an inevitable outcome.

Talbot Remembered

There are two monuments on the battlefield. The first, erected in 1888 on the north side of the D936 below the Horable and overlooking the battlefield, commemorates the French victory. The second, erected in 1953 on the site of a chapel, which no longer exists, and traditionally in the place where Shrewsbury had died and close to the Ford of Rosan on the bank of the Dordogne, commemorates the five hundredth anniversary of the battle. Shrewsbury's body was buried on the battlefield but towards the end of the fifteenth century it was brought back to England by his son, Sir Gilbert Talbot, and his tomb can today be seen in the Church of Saint Alkmund at Whitchurch in Shropshire.

The Talbot memorial erected in 1953:

In this place died General J. Talbot.

THE BATTLE OF CASTILLON, 17 JULY 1453

The church of Saint Alkmund in Whitchurch, Shropshire. The Earl of Shrewsbury's embalmed heart was buried under the porch and his bones in a tomb surmounted by his effigy in armour and with his feet resting on his dogs. The church was rebuilt in 1711–12 after the collapse of the fourteenth century tower. (Charles Singleton)

10

The End of English Aquitaine

The Advance Along the Dordogne

With the loss of the Earl of Shrewsbury and the rout of his army, the presence of the French army at Castillon, those of Clermont and Foix in the Médoc, and a fourth still in reserve with King Charles VII, now at Angoulême, perhaps the remaining Anglo-Gascon forces might have been expected to collapse rapidly. However, a number of towns and fortresses continued to hold out.

The day after the French victory at Castillon the siege of the town and castle had been renewed, and the garrison surrendered four days later. From Castillon the French progressed towards Bordeaux. The next town to fall was Saint-Emillion, only seven miles to the west. Saint-Emilion had a castle and was well protected by a perimeter wall and ditches. In theory, it could be defended by a small garrison with the support of the town militia. In the event, however, after the recent events at Castillon, the defenders had no appetite for a fight and quickly came to an arrangement to surrender the town.

Three miles further towards Bordeaux was the town of Libourne. With the arrival of the French army fresh from their victory and the surrender of Saint-Emilion, the inhabitants of Libourne initially defended the town, sallying out to attack a detachment charged with observation of one of the town's gates. The arrival of Charles VII, probably around 21 July having left Angoulême on 19 July, resulted in a rethink for the inhabitants and they decided to seek a composition for surrender. They argued that when the French had taken control of Bordeaux and Gascony in 1451, Libourne had been garrisoned and that on the arrival of Shrewsbury the inhabitants had tried to persuade the French garrison to remain to deny repossession of the town by the English. The garrison had, however, withdrawn abandoning the population who thus had no other choice than to accept, reluctantly, the return of English rule. If the garrison had remained to defend them, they went on to plead, they would, of course, have remained loyal to Charles.

Whether or not he believed this story is impossible to say, but it suited his politics to be merciful and the town was granted generous terms. Next to surrender was Fronsac, less than two miles to the west of Libourne. The garrison was allowed to leave.

Charles VII continued his advance towards Bordeaux. The King took up residence at the castle of Montferrant, about six miles northeast of the city and on the opposite bank of the Garonne, in the modern suburb of Bassens. A little to the south-west in Lormont the French constructed a bastille as an encampment for part of the army. Having set up the bastille, Charles VII set off with elements of his army to join the siege of Cadillac, 20 miles south-east of Bordeaux on the Garonne. Several small settlements and fortresses in the Entre-Deux-Mers between the Garonne and the Dordogne were either captured or surrendered.[1]

The Médoc

With the arrival of Charles VII on the banks of the Garonne opposite Bordeaux, one might expect that the Gascon will to resist would have crumbled, but this was not the case. In the Médoc, south into the Landes, and in the towns along the Garonne valley, resistance continued. While the army of de Beuil, de Chabannes, and Bureau had been approaching Castillon along the Dordogne, Clermont had been active in the Médoc. On 14 July he arrived before Castelnau-de-Médoc, 18 miles north-west of Bordeaux. Many of the men-at-arms from the Médoc had joined Talbot's army before the Battle of Castillon and Anglo-Gascon troops remaining in the region were thin on the ground. Castelnau held out for 15 days, but when the news of the defeat at Castillon and the progress of the French along the Dordogne reached the population, the town surrendered. Next the castle of Lesparre-Médoc fell, the only serious resistance remaining in the Médoc. There was no attempt by the French to win hearts and minds, since they knew that the local population was hostile to them. In return, they did not differentiate between the nobles, who remained loyal to the English cause, their vassals and the peasantry. They were all English to all intents and purposes, and crops, stores, and vineyards were destroyed; however, this was not simply indiscriminate destruction, it also served to deny the population and garrison of Bordeaux supplies. Religious establishments did not escape the scorched earth policy and numerous churches were sacked or burnt. Fortresses were razed to the ground, and some settlements disappeared from the map forever. Atrocities against women and children were recorded. The savagery of this period remained alive in popular memory for generations.

With resistance in the Médoc largely eliminated, Clermont was free to pursue the reduction of other towns and fortresses still in Anglo-Gascon

---

1   Ribadieu, *Histoire de la Conquête de la Guyenne par les Français*, pp.315–18.

hands. He moved south, leaving a detachment of Scots commanded by Robin Petit-Loup to secure the Médoc.²

Blanquefort

The places remaining in Anglo-Gascon hands included Rions, Saint-Macaire, Cadillac and Langon on the Garonne, Benauge in the Entre-Deux-Mers, and Villandraut in the Landes. First, however, there was the castle at Blanquefort, seven miles north of Bordeaux and important for the defence of the city. Clermont approached the fortress with a small detachment hoping to take the garrison by surprise, but he was to be disappointed. The castle itself was strong, with a keep with six towers, and an outer bailey with fortified towers and only one entrance – over the river Jalle to the south. The area adjacent to the river and surrounding the fortress was marshy and provided a natural defence. Gaillard de Duras, Lord of Blanquefort, had avoided capture at Castillon and returned to the castle to prepare its defence. When Clermont arrived, he found Blanquefort well garrisoned, well stocked with supplies and munitions, and equipped with artillery. After several fruitless attacks incurring a number of casualties, he decided to divide his army. He remained at Blanquefort while the Count of Foix, along with the Viscount of Lautrec, Poton de Xaintrailles, and the Lord of Albret moved south to attack the remaining places on the Garonne and in the Landes.³

The ruins of the fortress of Blanquefort. Built on a rocky outcrop, surrounded by marsh land it controlled the ancient Roman road from the Médoc to Bordeaux. (© Groupe d'Archéologie et d'Histoire de Blanquefort).

---

2   Ribadieu, *Histoire de la Conquête de la Guyenne par les Français,* pp.318–323. Monstrelet, *Chroniques,* vol.13, pp.132–134.
3   Ribadieu, *Histoire de la Conquête de la Guyenne par les Français,* pp.329–330.

THE END OF ENGLISH AQUITAINE

The Garonne

The army of the Count of Foix quickly took Saint-Macaire, which surrendered to Poton de Xaintrailles, while Langon and, after a half-hearted defence, the castle of Villandraut capitulated to Albret. There were left only Cadillac, Rions, two miles north-west, and the castle of Benauge in the modern commune of Arbis, three miles north-east of the town, to deal with.

Cadillac had a mixed Anglo-Gascon garrison commanded by a Gascon captain, Gaillardet. As at Blanquefort, where Duras had put the time at his disposal to good use, Gaillardet had prepared for a siege. Cadillac consisted of a castle and a walled town, protected by deep ditches. A stream ran round the walls of the castle and the north of the town before joining the Garonne, which runs to the west of the town. The Garonne was only 200 metres from the walls and, thus, gave no room to manoeuvre for an army without coming under fire from the walls. However, there was a gate in the wall facing the river and only one large tower on the walls. Gaillardet judged that the ramparts on this side were not sufficiently strong, and that, even with the limited manoeuvring space for the besiegers, it was here that the attack would come, and he constructed earthworks before the gate and the tower facing the Garonne. Behind this construction of wooden beams and earth he placed his archers. The defences were sufficiently daunting for Foix and Lautrec to call for artillery. Bureau obliged by sending a number of bombards from Lormont.

While these bombards were being deployed Gaillardet decided to abandon the earthworks and withdraw within the town's walls. Before doing so, however, he set the timber alight, hoping that this would prevent the use of the defence works by the French. However, the French appreciated the value of the earthworks, extinguished the fire and advanced their guns, protected by the earthworks, to fire on the walls from point-blank range. The guns quickly had an effect and on 19 September 1453, the walls having been breached, an assault was launched with faggots of wood thrown into the ditches to allow the troops to cross. The fighting was hard, but the French were able to take possession of the town, six weeks after the start of the siege. Gaillardet and those of the garrison that could do so retired to the castle.

The southern gate of Cadillac and a section of the town walls and a tower. The defences were constructed in the early fourteenth century and there was a ditch in front of the walls with a drawbridge protecting the entry to the gate. The commander of the garrison constructed earthworks in front of the gate to reinforce the defences. When the earthworks were abandoned by the garrison the French advanced their guns to fire point-blank at the walls to open a breach. (Peter Hoskins)

Towards the end of the month the situation in the castle was becoming desperate and Bureau's artillery was having an effect. The garrison called for terms, offering 10,000 *écus* and the surrender of the town if they were granted their freedom. Charles VII, who seems to have been shuttling between Saint-Macaire and Montferrant to supervise the siege at Bordeaux, which had begun on 1 August, and the progress at Cadillac, replied that he had no need of their money and that the only terms on offer were to surrender at his mercy. With more and more breaches appearing in the walls, the garrison had no option but to do so. Gaillardet paid the ultimate price for his loyalty to Henry VI and his determined defence and was beheaded. Under the terms of the surrender of Cadillac the castles at Rions and Benauge were also supposed to open their gates to the French, but for the time being refused to do so. Other than these two small fortresses all that now remained in the hands of the Anglo-Gascons were Bordeaux and Blanquefort.[4]

The Siege and Fall of Bordeaux

The siege of Bordeaux is recorded as opening on 1 August 1453. Although by now the Anglo-Gascons held only a handful of places, Bordeaux was going to be a tough nut to crack. Bounded to the east by the Garonne, the city covered 365 acres, was surrounded by walls six feet thick and with a perimeter of almost four miles. The walls were pierced by numerous gates, many protected by barbicans and the remainder with towers. Some of these gates were minor, in some cases authorised to allow merchants access to the quays on the Garonne. In time of emergency, the city authorities could order these openings to be walled up, and presumably that was the case on this occasion. There was also a substantial fleet of English and Gascon ships in the port of Bordeaux. To man these impressive defences there were reported to be 4,000 English soldiers and 4,000 Gascons in the garrison.

Across the Garonne at Lormont the French could observe the movements in the town, but with the river more than 600 yards wide the city was out of effective artillery range. There were no bridges over the river near Bordeaux in the Middle Ages, and access to Bordeaux was either by sea or by land after moving upstream on the right bank of the Garonne before crossing and moving north towards the Médoc. Clermont's troops besieging Blanquefort, the laying waste of the Médoc, and a detachment of troops in the Landes made resupply over land problematic for Bordeaux. Charles VII had anticipated the importance of cutting off supply from England, and at the start of the campaign had ordered the assembly of a fleet in the Gironde estuary. Ships had been brought from The Low Countries,

---

4   Ribadieu, *Histoire de la Conquête de la Guyenne par les Français,* pp.330–332 & 342-343. Chartier, *Chronique de Charles VII, Roi de* France, vol.3, pp.9–14. Monstrelet, *Chroniques,* vol.13, pp.134–136.

Brittany, Normandy, and Spain and now moved upstream to Bordeaux. This fleet was immediately attacked by the Bordelais and to protect it the bastille at Lormont was extended to give it shelter. This certainly kept the Bordelais at bay, but as one of the French commanders, Jean de Beuil, observed it was all very well to have built the bastille, but it could be seen as a sign of weakness. The besiegers risked being besieged themselves and exposed their vulnerability. A bastille also diminished the confidence of the troops, for as stated by de Beuil: 'A bastille never has the value of the fortifications of a town … I think they have been of little use where they have been constructed, and I have seen the bad effects in English sieges at Orléans, Compiègne, Dieppe, and Mont-Saint-Michel.'[5] The bastille garrison was 1,500 to 1,600 lances, archers, and artillery.

In response to the French bastille the Bordelais built a similar structure on the left bank of the Garonne. The location of this bastille has been a matter of speculation but may have been near the current Quai de Bacalan about two miles upstream from Lormont. The Anglo-Gascon crews, with the advantage of local knowledge of tides and currents, sallied forth to make frequent attacks on the French bastille and shipping and then returned to shelter under the protection of the guns in Bordeaux. Much as de Beuil had feared, the French were compelled to focus a great deal of their effort on defending their bastille. During these raids the Bordelais tried to take prisoners, either with an eye on ransoms or as hostages in the event of the eventual fall of the city.

The defence of Bordeaux was led by Roger Lord Camoys, appointed Seneschal of the Duchy of Aquitaine on 4 July 1453.[6] Under his command were a number of English and Gascon nobles, including the Lord of Lesparre who had been among those who urged the English to return to Gascony in 1453. The siege had been under way for almost two months when the news came to Bordeaux of the surrender of Cadillac. This, following the earlier fall of Saint-Macaire, removed any last lingering hope of supplies coming downstream on the Garonne. Famine was beginning to make itself felt and divisions were appearing between the English and the Gascons. The former had less to fear from the vengeance of Charles VII than the latter, who risked accusations of treachery, and they were showing increasing reluctance to fight. Lord Camoys had removed all the cordage from the English ships to discourage desertion, and the English soldiery, even if against their will, remained at their posts. However, the division between the Gascons who wished to fight on and many of the English who simply want to return home became more evident as the situation deteriorated.

With the fall of Cadillac, Duras, who had been holding out in Blanquefort for two months, decided that it was hopeless to continue the struggle. He asked for safe conduct to negotiate the surrender of the castle, but this was refused by Charles VII. He was well aware that he faced the risk of execution

---

5 Ribadieu, *Histoire de la Conquête de la Guyenne par les Français,* pp.337–338.
6 Gascon Rolls, gasconrolls.org, C61/139, Membrane 3-66.

for having supported the return of the English, and he decided to make his way to Bordeaux. Before doing so, however, he negotiated an agreement with the Count of Clermont providing for the safety of the English in his garrison; he then made his way secretly across the marshes to Bordeaux.

The news that Duras brought with him of the surrender of Blanquefort hastened the change of spirit among the Bordelais. A consequence of the fall of Cadillac and Blanquefort was that the artillery from these two places was redeployed to add to the bombardment of the city from the sides unprotected by the Garonne. This, and the increasing problem of hunger, led the Bordelais to ask Charles VII for safe conduct to treat for the capitulation of Bordeaux. In early October a deputation of nobles, churchmen and other city notables were granted safe conduct to treat with Charles VII at Montferrant castle. They offered to surrender Bordeaux in exchange for their lives and the right to retain their possessions. The King replied to the effect that if that was all that they had to say then they may as well return to the city under safe conduct. He said that in view of their offences he could not, and would not, grant their request for clemency. He was determined to take possession of the town and all those within together with their possessions and that the citizens within must submit to his mercy. Those that had broken their oaths could expect to be punished both as an example to others and to serve as a reminder about good conduct in the future.

Meanwhile Jean Bureau had been selecting emplacements for the artillery free from Cadillac and Blanquefort and told the King that he was confident that he could force the surrender of the city. The Bordelais continued to attack the French fleet and positions from the Garonne, but the French brought 16 additional ships from La Rochelle. With their strengthened fleet the French posed a serious threat to the bastille of Bordeaux. If it were to fall the vulnerability of the city to attack would be greatly increased. Finding a settlement was becoming increasingly urgent, but the question was how to proceed after the rebuff suffered during the meeting with the King when he had seemed intransigent.

One of the commanders of the French army was Joachim Rouhault. After the surrender of Bordeaux in 1451 he had been appointed Constable of Bordeaux and he was seen by the Bordelais as a potentially sympathetic go-between with the King. At the request of the representatives of the inhabitants, Roger Camoys contacted Rouhault and invited him to come into Bordeaux for talks. Rouhault reported the request to the King who authorised him to open preliminary talks. The discussions in Bordeaux were sufficiently encouraging for a further meeting to be arranged, this time at the French bastille at Lormont, with 25 to 30 Anglo-Gascon representatives. The two sides were still far apart at the end of the day. Camoys continued to ask for an amnesty for all and the right for inhabitants to retain their possessions. The French representatives replied that, in view of the offences of the Gascons, these terms were unacceptable. No progress was made, and talks were adjourned until the next day.

On the second day progress was finally made: the Bordelais offered, in return for their lives and retention of possessions, to renounce all their privileges and pay an indemnity of 100,000 *écus*. The French demanded that 20 men within the city, considered to be the Gascon leaders of the rebellion, be handed over at the King's mercy, implicitly accepting that the lives and possessions of others would be guaranteed. These 20 men were amongst the Gascons, both military and civilian, who were considered guilty of handing Gascony back to the English. Camoys was well aware that this amounted to a death sentence for the men concerned, who faced decapitation or hanging. The French terms were refused, and the talks broke up again without agreement.

However, with conditions continuing to deteriorate within the city, on Tuesday 9 October, a further Anglo-Gascon embassy, again headed by Camoys, went to negotiate with the French. On this occasion they were received by Charles VII at Montferrant castle. Camoys repeated his plea for the lives and possessions of the people within the city and offered again to renounce their privileges and pay 100,000 *écus*. The King ordered the Anglo-Gascons to withdraw while he consulted with his advisers. Opinion was divided: some called for a withdrawal of the concessions already made and demanded an unconditional surrender at the mercy of the King. Others pleaded for a generous settlement, in part to avoid leaving simmering resistance, which might lead to a future uprising. Those who favoured a settlement also pointed out that an epidemic raging in the French camp was costing lives and the sooner the army could disperse the better.[7] The King may have been eager to bring the siege to an end, but equally he was keen to arrest those whom he saw as being principally responsible for the uprising after the treaty of 1451 and the return of Shrewsbury and the English.

The Anglo-Gascon ambassadors were recalled. They were bitterly disappointed to find that the King still required the surrender of the 20 men whom he considered to be guilty of a breach of their oaths and having betrayed him to the English. Camoys and his companions refused in any circumstances to send their comrades in arms to a certain death. After a heated discussion the King relented; the 20 would not be executed but must go into permanent exile and forfeit their lands in France. All French prisoners held in Bordeaux, whether or not they had agreed to pay ransoms, were to be freed without ransom. The previously proposed payment of 100,000 *écus* was confirmed. The privileges granted under the 1451 treaty were abolished: Bordeaux would henceforth be unable to mint coinage, vote taxes, hold a parliament, or refuse military service. Some notable Gascons, faced with the loss of historic privileges, asked for the liberty to go into exile but keep their possessions. Charles granted the request but, perhaps fearful of a major exodus of wealth, for a maximum of 40 men; any donations of

---

7   It had been suggested that Jacques de Chabannes, who died on 20 October 1453, may have been the victim of plague. However, dysentery was a very common disease in siege armies in view of the insanitary conditions in a siege camp. The siege of Bordeaux had been going on for 10 weeks, and it is highly likely that the army was beset by dysentery fever.

property or legacies to family members who remained would be respected. The population that remained were required to swear never to again rise in rebellion and to remain loyal to Charles VII and the French Crown.

The agreement was signed at Montferrant on 9 October, and three days later 12 hostages, six English and six Gascon, were handed over to the French to guarantee the treaty. On 14 October the Bordeaux bastille was handed over to the French. The city itself should have been handed over two days later, but there seem to have been last minute doubts among the garrison and an incident arose, although no details are recorded about it, which led to the handover being deferred three days. On Friday 19 October, the gates were finally opened to the French. The English departed with full military honours and were escorted to their ships by French heralds, free to leave for either England or Calais. Charles VII chose not to make a ceremonial entry into Bordeaux but left for Tours. The King did not intend to risk another rebellion, and the Count of Clermont was appointed the King's Lieutenant-General with a body of men-at-arms and archers to secure the city and duchy. Jean Bureau was appointed Mayor of Bordeaux.

Despite the fall of Bordeaux, the garrisons of the fortresses of Benauge and Rions, which should have been surrendered under the terms of the capitulation of Cadillac at the end of September, still held out. They maintained that they could only surrender on the authority of King Henry VI. Charles VII sent troops and by the end of the month this last hopeless resistance was over.[8]

---

8 Ribadieu, *Histoire de la Conquête de la Guyenne par les Français,* pp.333–356, Chartier, *Chronique de Charles VII, Roi de* France, vol.3, pp.14–19.

11

Aftermath

The attachment of the Duchy of Aquitaine to the Kings of England had begun in 1152 with the marriage of Eleanor of Aquitaine to Henry Plantagenet, two years later King Henry II of England. After more than three centuries the duchy, which had been the cause of so much discord between the two realms, passed definitively to the French Crown. Henceforth the duchy was held in direct rule by French Kings, save for two short periods later in the fifteenth century and in the eighteenth century. Of the once extensive English holdings in France only the Calais Pale remained. Charles VII considered an expedition to take this remaining enclave. However, the Calais Pale was surrounded by Burgundian territory and a French campaign to take the town would entail crossing land held by the Duke of Burgundy. Additionally, after an abortive attempt to take Calais by siege in 1436 the Duke of Burgundy had concluded a truce with England in 1439, and this was still in force in 1453. Faced with the risk of provoking a war with Burgundy, Charles VII elected not to try to take this last stronghold.[1] Calais was to remain in English hands for more than another century, finally falling to the French in 1558 during the reign of Queen Mary I. However, the Arms of the English, and subsequently British, monarchs continued to incorporate the *fleur de lys*, symbolising the continuing claim to the French Crown, which had been a primary cause of the Hundred Years' War, until the Treaty of Amiens in 1801.

The change of regime not only entailed political changes with the absorption of Aquitaine, or Guyenne as it was known to the French, into the Kingdom of France but also brought heraldic changes. The arms of the Dukes of Aquitaine before the attachment to the English Crown had comprised a lion rampant in red on a white background[2]. In the late twelve century Richard the Lionheart adopted three gold lions passant on a red background as his royal arms, which is still the arms of England[3]. This may

---

1   Monstrelet, *Chroniques*, vol.13, p.138.
2   Passant guardant or - on a red field, three gold lions.
3   In heraldic terms: on a field argent a lion rampant gules.

have been an amalgamation of his father Henry II's arms of two lions with the single lion of Aquitaine. Strictly speaking there were no separate arms for the Duchy of Aquitaine during the period when the kings of England held the title. When Charles, younger brother of King Louis XI, was created Duke of Aquitaine in 1469, he adopted arms with the *fleur de lys* quartered for France with one gold lion rampant on a red background, thus reverting to the historical symbol of a single lion for Aquitaine[4].

Much was to change for Bordeaux. It had been a great city within the English sphere of influence, and its wine trade with England was so important that Louis XI was to say: 'If the city of Bordeaux is one of the biggest and best populated cities of the realm it owes it to the island of England ... The English brought their gold and silver which they converted into the wines of Gascony.'[5] Its importance had been such that a Christian monk on a mission for the sovereign of Persia in 1282, visiting Bordeaux and considering it to be the capital of England, decided to forgo a visit to England itself.[6] It now passed finally to the Kingdom of France. The arms of the town during the attachment to the English Crown, certainly from the fifteenth century, had incorporated the three lions of England over an image of one of the gates of the town; the town had never, however, adopted the *fleur de lys* after Edward III laid claim to the French Crown on the grounds that the duchy was not part of France. Following the expulsion of the English the three lions were replaced by a single lion and the *fleurs de lys* were added.[7]

The changes were profound for Bordeaux. The loss of traditional privileges entailed the loss of the considerable autonomy that the town had had. Charles VII was determined to prevent any further attempts of a return of the English and set about constructing two fortresses: the Fort du Hâ and the Castle of the Trompette within Bordeaux. Although partly to discourage a return by the English they were also there to ensure control of a potentially rebellious population.

For the Gascons the departure of the English was a moment of crisis. Many had become immersed in English life over the centuries. Many had intermarried, merchants had built prosperous businesses based on trade with England, and nobles had been members of the Order of the Garter. Civilians and military personalities had been closely involved in the government of the duchy. The frontiers of Gascony had fluctuated considerably over three centuries and similarly there had been shifting

---

4   D'azure semé de *fleurs de liys* d'or quartered with gules a lion rampant or.
5   Jean-Marc Soyez, *Quand les Anglaise Vendangeaient l'Aquitaine* (Paris: Fayard, 1979), p.245.
6   J. M. Tourneur-Aumont, *La Bataille de Poitiers (1356) et la Construction de la France* (Poitiers: Université de Poitiers, 1943), p.31.
7   Guilhem Pépin, *Les Emblèmes Historique de l'Aquitaine,* https://aquitaine-historique.com/images/Site/Guilhem/Guilhem%20Pepin%20-%20Les%20emblemes%20historiques%20de%20l'Aquitaine.pdf. Meaudre de Lapouyade, *Les Armoiries de Bordeaux* (Bordeaux: Gounouilhou, 1913), pp.18 and 21.

allegiances within some families, but others, notably the de Grailly family, had been loyal throughout this long period. Difficult decisions now had to be taken by many.

In addition to the 20 banished after the surrender of Bordeaux and compelled to go to into exile, and the 40 authorised to leave, many others left clandestinely, travelling either overland or leaving by sea from the Atlantic coast. In addition to going to England, Gascons were subsequently to be found in Catalonia, Navarre, Béarn, Italy, Aragon, and Brittany. It has been estimated that at least 2,000 Gascons emigrated to England. They were almost entirely drawn from the nobility or merchant class. Very few were men of the church, craftsmen, or peasants. For the nobility there was the question of oaths given to the King of England and commitment to the concept of an Aquitaine separate from France; for the merchants there was often the belief that they could make their fortunes with the wine trade which they were confident would continue.

The emigrants left in two waves, the first going after the surrender of Bordeaux and the remainder from 1454 after a campaign of repression triggered by an abortive attempt to encourage a return of the English. Of those who went to England some were to remain and build new lives and families, while others in due course returned to France and, having sworn oaths to the King, were accepted back without punishment. Somewhat paradoxically among nobles who eventually chose to return some did so not because they had come to accept willingly the change of regime but rather out of disgust that the English had abandoned all pretence of a return to France.[8]

Among the exiles was Jean de Foix-Grailly, Earl of Kendal. He had gone into exile in 1451 but returned to fight with Talbot, was then captured at Castillon and imprisoned. His father had to sell lordships in Savoy to pay part of his ransom to secure his freedom in 1460. He went to England, but his stay was short-lived and, after finding himself on the wrong side at the Battle of Northampton in 1461, returned to France. In return for his swearing allegiance to the French Crown, Louis XI obliged Olivier de Coëtivy to renounce the remainder of his ransom and restored his lands to him having bought them back from Gaston IV, Count of Foix. Galliard de Durfort, who had been among those banished and had forfeited his possessions in Aquitaine, subsequently gave loyal service to the English Crown but in 1476 returned to France, swore allegiance to Louis XI and had his possessions returned to him. Pierre de Montferrant, Lord of Lesparre, was less fortunate; having been banished in 1453 he had kept in touch with events in Bordeaux. Hearing of discontent because of a tax imposed on wine he decided that the time was ripe for another rising. He returned in June 1454 with other exiles in the hope of stirring up rebellion. He travelled

---

8 A. Peyrègne, 'Les Émigrés Gascons en Angleterre (1453–1485)' in *Annales du Midi: revue archéologique historique et philiologique de la France méridionale*, vol.66, No.26, 1954, pp.113–128.

with a safe conduct under the pretence of having business to attend to. Nevertheless, he was quickly captured and sent to Poitiers for trial; there was to be no mercy this time. His safe conduct was declared false, he was decapitated, and his body cut into six pieces to be impaled above the gates of the city.[9]

The French remained concerned about an English attempt to return to France, but there were too many problems at home for that to be a realistic prospect. Political divisions and social discontent were simmering and within two years of the English defeat at Castillon the First Battle of St Albans opened the Wars of the Roses, which were to pre-occupy England for the next 30 years. The Anglo-Gascon Duchy of Aquitaine was gone forever.

---

9   Chartier, *Chronique de Charles VII, Roi de France*, vol.3, pp.49–50. Ribadieu, *Histoire de la Conquête de la Guyenne par les Français*, pp.377–381.

Colour Plate Commentaries

Plate A

John Talbot, Earl of Shrewsbury, had sworn an oath when released from French captivity in 1450 never again to wage war against King Charles VII. He honoured his oath and rode into battle unarmed and without armour. Towards the end of the battle Talbot's horse was struck and killed by a ball fired from a culverin or serpentine. He was unseated and he was trapped by the body of his horse which fell upon him. He was finished off by a French archer with a sword or dagger thrust to the throat.

Plate B

Thomas Everingham, the Earl of Shrewsbury's standard bearer, dismounted along with the other men-at-arms. He advanced to place the earl's standard in the ground by the French artillery park as the signal for the assault to begin.

Plate C

A French crossbowman. Despite the advances with hand-held firearms, the crossbow was still widely used.

Plate D

Jean Bureau, the architect of the development of French artillery, was one of the commanders of the army which defeated the Anglo-Gascon army at Castillon. Here he is portrayed urging his men on.

Plate E

1
The Royal Arms of England during the reign of Henry VI, carried into battle at Castillon by the Anglo-Gascon army. Edward III first quartered the lions of England with the *fleurs de lys* of France when he formalised his claim to the French throne in 1340. This form was adopted by Henry IV in 1399.

2

The arms of John Talbot, First Earl of Shrewsbury, carried to the French camp by Thomas Everingham to signal the start of the Anglo-Gascon attack on the French camp at Castillon.

Plate F

1

The Trinity banner, also displayed by Henry V's army at Agincourt, and carried into battle by the Anglo-Gascon army.

2

The arms of Jean V de Bueil, one of the French commanders at Castillon and twice wounded in the fighting. He went on to play an important part in the subsequent siege of Bordeaux.

Plate G

1

The arms of Jean IV de Châtillon, Count of Penthièvre, appointed by Charles VII as commander of the French army in Gascony in 1450 and present as a commander at Castillon.

2

The arms of Jacques V de Chabannes one of the French commanders at Castillon. Wounded at the battle he died on 20 October 1453 after the siege of Bordeaux, possibly of his wounds or the plague, but more probably of dysentery contracted during the siege.

Plate H

1

The arms of Jean de Foix-Grailly, Viscount of Castillon and Earl of Kendal. The Grailly family had long been loyal to the kings of England. Jean went into exile in England after the surrender of Bordeaux in 1451. He subsequently returned for the campaign of 1452–3. He was captured when Castillon fell after the battle. He was held prisoner until 1460 when he was ransomed. He left once again for England only to return to France in 1461 where he swore allegiance to Charles VII.

2

The arms of Jean Bureau, along with his brother Gaspard the architect of the French development of artillery. He was present at the Battle of Castillon and played an important role throughout the campaigns to expel the English from France. He was of bourgeois origins but knighted in 1447.

Bibliography

Books

Autrand, Françoise, *Charles V : le Sage* (Paris: Fayard, 1994)
Barker, Juliet, *Conquest, The English Kingdom of France, 1417–50* (London: Little, Brown, 2009)
Basin, Thomas (Tr. and notes), Blanchard, Joël, Collard, Franck, and de Kisch, Yves, *Histoire de Charles VII et Louis XI* (Paris: Éditions Pocket, 2018)
Beuil, Jean de, Ed. Lecestre, Léon, *Le Jouvencal*, vol. 1 (Paris: Renouard, 1887)
Bouvier, Gilles le, (Alain Chartier ed.), *L'Histoire Mémorable des Grands Troubles de ce Royaume sous le Roi Charles VII* (Nevers: Pierre Roussin, 1594)
Brissaud, D, *Les Anglais en Guyenne* (Paris: J.-B. Dumoulin, 1875)
Bully, Philippe, *Charles VII, le "Rois des Merveilles"* (Paris: Tallendier, 1994)
Chartier, Jean, (Vallet de Viriville ed.) *Chronique de Charles VII, Roi de France*, vol. 2 and vol. 3 (Paris: P Jannet, 1858)
Crouy-Chanel, Emmanuel de, *Canons Médiévaux, Puissance du Feu* (Paris: Rempart, 2010)
Deviosse, Jean, *Jean le Bon* (Paris: Fayard, 1985)
Enguerrand de Monstrelet, *Chroniques*, (J. A. Buchon ed.), vols.10, 11, 12 and 13 (Paris: Verdière, 1826)
Favier, Jean, *La Guerre de Cent Ans* (Paris: Fayard, 1981)
Fresne de Beaucourt, G. du, *Histoire de Charles VII*, vol.5, *Le Roi Victorieux 1449–53* (Paris: Alphonse Picard, 1890)
Hoskins, Peter, *Siege Warfare During the Hundred Years' War* (Barnsley: Pen & Sword, 2018)
Lapouyade, Meaudre de, *Les Armoiries de Bordeaux* (Bordeaux: Gounouilhou, 1913)
Leseur, Guillaume, (Henri Courteault ed.), *Histoire de Gaston IV, Comte de Foix*, vols 1 and 2 (Paris: Renouard, 1893 & 1897)
Nicolle, David, *The Fall of English France 1449–53* (Oxford: Osprey, 2012)
Pollard, A. J., *John Talbot and the War in France, 1427–1453* (Barnsley: Pen & Sword, 2005)

Ribadieu, Henry, *Histoire de la Conquête de la Guyenne par les Français de ses Antécédents et ses Suits* (Bordeaux: Paul Chaumas, 1866)

Rogers, Clifford J., *War Cruel and Sharp, English Strategy Under Edward III, 1327–1360* (Woodbridge: The Boydell Press, 2000)

Rose, Susan, *Calais, An English Town in France, 1347–1558* (Woodbridge: The Boydell Press, 2008)

Soyez, Jean-Marc, *Quand les Anglaise Vendangeaient l'Aquitaine* (Paris: Fayard, 1979)

Tourneur-Aumont, J.M. *La Bataille de Poitiers (1356) et la Construction de la France* (Poitiers: Université de Poitiers, 1943)

Articles

Burne, A. H., 'The French Camp at Castillon' in *The Royal Engineers Journal*, vol. LXII (December 1948), pp.290–1

Dubled, H, 'L'Artillerie Royale Française à l'Epoque de Charles VII at au Début du Règne de Louis XI (1437–1469) Les Frères Bureau' in *Sciences et Techniques de l'Armement, Mémorial de l'Artillerie Française*, 50:4 (1976), pp.555–637

Peyrègne, A., 'Les Émigrés Gascons en Angleterre (1453–1485)' in *Annales du Midi: Revue Archéologique Historique et Philologique de la France Méridionale*, vol.66, No.26, 1954, pp.113–128.

Miscellaneous

Nicolas, Matthieu, *La Dynastie des Grailly : une famille noble au cœur de la guerre de Cent Ans* (Toulouse: Université Toulouse Jean Jaurès, 2017), doctoral thesis

Les plus Anciens Recits de la Bataille de Castillon (Castillon: Le Groupe de Recherches Historiques et de Sauvetages Archéologiques du Castillonnais, undated), collection of documents relating to the Battle of Castillon.

About the author

Peter Hoskins served in the Royal Air Force before turning to historical research and writing. He has written widely on the Hundred Years' War: *In the Steps of the Black Prince, The Road to Poitiers, 1355–1356; Agincourt 1415, A Tourist's Guide to the Campaign; Crécy 1346, A Tourists' Guide; Siege Warfare in the Hundred Years' War* and *Generalship In The Hundred Years' war: The Black Prince and King Jean II of France*. His most recent book *A Legion Para in Algeria*, Tony Hunter-Choat's War, 1957–62, published by Helion in 2022, covered the Algerian War though the eyes of a much-decorated British para in the French Foreign Legion.

About the artists

Giorgio Albertini was born in 1968 in Milan where he still lives. After studying Medieval History at the University of Milan, he become involved in archaeology and has been involved in several excavations for European institutions. He was responsible for the graphic depiction of archaeological sites and finds. He also works as a historical and scientific illustrator for many institutions, museums, and magazines such as *National Geographic Magazine, BBC History,* and *Medieval Warfare*. He has always been interested in military history and is one of the founders of *"Focus Wars"* magazine.

Born in Curitiba, in southern Brazil, Anderson Subtil holds a degree in Drawing from the School of Music and Fine Arts of the Paraná State. Since 2018, he has worked as an illustrator for several Helion & Company Series. His artworks have been published in books and magazines in Brazil, the United States, the United Kingdom, France, Austria and Japan.

Other titles in the From Retinue to Regiment series:

No 1 *Richard III and the Battle of Bosworth* Mike Ingram

No 2 *Tanaka 1587: Japan's Greatest Unknown Samurai Battle* Stephen Turnbull

No 3 *The Army of the Swabian League 1525* Doug Miller

No 4 *The Italian Wars Volume 1: The Expedition of Charles VIII into Italy and the Battle of Fornovo* Massimo Predonzani & Alberici Vincenzo, translated by Irene Maccolini

No 5 *The Commotion Time: Tudor Rebellion in the West, 1549* E.T. Fox

No 6 *The Italian Wars Volume 2: Agnadello 1509, Ravenna 1512, Marignano 1515* Massimo Predonzani & Alberici Vincenzo, translated by Rachele Tiso

No 7 *The Tudor Arte of Warre Volume 1: The Conduct of War from Henry VII to Mary I, 1485-1558* Jonathan Davies

No 8 *The Ethiopian-Adal War 1529-1543: The Conquest of Abyssinia* Jeffrey M. Shaw

No 9 *The Ōnin War: A Turning Point in Samurai History* Stephen Turnbull

No 10 *One Faith, One Law, One King: French Armies of the Wars of Religion 1562–1598* T J O'Brien de Clare

No 11 *The Italian Wars Volume 3: Francis I and the Battle of Pavia 1525* Massimo Predonzani & Alberici Vincenzo

No 12 *On the Borderlands of Great Empires: Transylvanian Armies 1541-1613* Florin Nicolae Ardelean

No 14 *The Art of Shooting Great Ordnance: A History of the Development, Manufacture and Use of Artillery, 1494–1628* Jonathan Davies

No 15 *The Italian Wars Volume 4: The Battle of Ceresole 1544 - The Crushing Defeat of the Imperial Army* Massimo Predonzani & Simon Miller

No 16 *The Men of Warre: The Clothes, Weapons and Accoutrements of the Scots at War 1460–1600* Jenn Scott

No 17 *The German Peasants' War 1524–26* Douglas Miller

No 18 *The Tudor Arte of Warre Volume 2: The conduct of war in the reign of Elizabeth I, 1558–1603: Diplomacy, Strategy, Campaigns and Battles* Jonathan Davies

No 19 *The Kalmar War 1611–1613: Gustavus Adolphus's First War* Michael Fredholm von Essen

No 20 *Hojo: Samurai Warlords 1487–1590* Stephen Turnbull

No 21 *The Battle of Castillon 1453: The Death Knell for English France* Peter Hoskins